# A Heart for Horses

## What Horses Want Humans to Know

# A Heart for Horses

## What Horses Want Humans to Know

Marina Parris and "Black Diamond"

Zug, Switzerland

Black Diamond Publishing, Switzerland

Cover design and interior book layout by Lorna Johnson, lornajohnson.com
Book production management by Ruth Schwartz, thewonderlady.com

Photos: Tamara Callstrom, Eponaquest Horses (Leyla and Savannah), Chatrigna Ferguson, Silvia Furter, Isabelle Guidicelli, Béatrice Hunkeler, Sladjana Ivanovic, Sandra Padrutt, Rikke de Romijn, Kathryn Rigert, Catherine Jane Schweizer, Isabel Steinhauser, Katja Stuppia (cover photo), and Sandra Teuber.

*A Heart for Horses: What Horses Want Humans to Know* by Marina Parris. -- 1st ed.
ISBN 978-3-9524795-7-5 paperback
ISBN 978-3-9524795-8-2 ebook

# Dedication

This book is dedicated to my horse Hummer (Black Diamond) and my horsemanship teacher Ronnie Willis.

I experienced the horse-human relationship in such a deep and profound way that it was often beyond any words. What I learned made me who I am today.

This book is also dedicated to horse people looking for a heart-based connection with their horses, open to learning about themselves through their horses and seeking to create a true partnership.

# Foreword

Marina may have found her way to horses later in life, but she arrived with an open heart and, in doing so, allowed the magical world of equines to transform her. When the exchange between horse and human comes from compassion, a deep relationship becomes possible. This happens, Marina tells us, when we are open to seeing things from the horse's perspective and willing to reflect on our own behavior.

I was delighted to read Marina's concise text, enjoying the clear progression through her philosophy and techniques, impressed with her practical advice and consistent dedication to educating horse people of all levels.

This outstanding book covers everything, from mindfulness and awareness of equine behavior to the details of handling and training of horses ridden under saddle and those that are not, perhaps used solely in equine-facilitated learning.

Marina often quotes the famous cowboys who grounded her early education with horses: Ronnie Willis, Ray Hunt, Tom and Bill Dorrance, and others who changed how horses on the North American continent are handled and trained. And she knew there was something exceptional about a horsewoman who produced one of the most ground-breaking equestrian books of all time—and one that had a profound effect on me as a mid-career hunter-jumper professional—Linda Kohanov.

Kohanov's Eponaquest Program was developed from her book and has evolved over several decades, giving rise to teachers like Marina worldwide.

Undoubtedly it was a significant decision for Marina to take an American Quarter Horse, Hummer, back to Europe with her. She did not want to lose such a unique connection. Hummer is one very fortunate boy to have found himself with this remarkable, caring horsewoman.

Horses need to lead a peaceful and productive life as close to their natural state as possible. They look forward to the kindnesses and generosity of those in their presence, feeding mind, body and soul with their energy and experiences.

Marina wraps it all up in *A Heart for Horses,* perfectly organized and readable by anyone of any age who loves horses and wants to know more.

My own book, *The Compassionate Equestrian,* was published seven years ago as of this writing. I am humbled by the advent of many more kind, understanding equestrians, coming forward to lead the way for a new generation of horse-lovers, placing heart-based approaches above the need to "get something" from the horse every time they spend time with it.

—Susan Gordon

*The Compassionate Equestrian* is Susan Gordon's first book. She began riding professionally in 1983 and trained eventing, hunter, jumper, and dressage horses, apprenticing with other top trainers such as the late Michael Patrick in her chosen disciplines. Susan now lives on Salt Spring Island, B.C., Canada.

# Acknowledgements

Thank you, dear reader, for buying this book and being open to how it may guide and inspire you on the journey with your horse.

I am very grateful to my father (†), who made it possible for me to change careers at 35, and to my mother and brother, who have always supported me in doing what I love.

A big thanks and appreciation go out to Ronnie Willis (†), who laid the foundation for how I interacted with horses, a way that helped me become a better human and helped me see the world through the eyes of a horse. I am also thankful to his lovely wife, Gina Willis, for allowing me to quote Ronnie, so that his wisdom could be shared with others.

My personal journey with horses has given me the opportunity to meet wonderful people whose work and lives have inspired me. One of these people is Linda Kohanov, whose work on emotional intelligence is an integral part of this book.

Putting what I learned and experienced over 20 years into this book was a team effort. Writing the text was one thing, getting feedback and proofreading another issue and with this Claudia Köfer and Phyllis Elving were a great help. Chatrigna Ferguson helped out with the photo selection, matching each picture with the text message.

I am very glad that the following people allowed me to use their picture(s) for this book: Tamara Callstrom, Eponaquest Horses (Leyla and Savannah), Chatrigna Ferguson, Silvia Furter, Isabelle Guidicelli, Béatrice Hunkeler, Sladjana Ivanovic, Sandra Padrutt, Rikke de Romijn, Kathryn Rigert, Catherine Jane Schweizer, Isabel Steinhauser, Katja Stuppia (cover photo), and Sandra Teuber.

Lorna Johnson then took all this content and turned it into the book you are holding in your hand. Ruth Schwartz coordinated this entire process in the background and ensured a smooth flow along the way. And it was my dear friend Eugene Kilgore who initially put me in touch with these lovely ladies.

# Contents

**"You are here to learn, the horse is just here to help you learn."**

—Ronnie Willis

# My Inspiration

This book came about because I felt that many riding books and lessons still focus too much on technique and outside aids and not enough on who the rider needs to become on the inside so that the horse chooses to become a willing partner.

What I learned from a horseman named Ronnie Willis in Montana back in 2004 laid the foundation for my work with horses, and later with people and horses. Sometimes I felt that his wisdom and that of the Quarter Horse named Hummer that I bought in Montana was flowing through my fingers as I wrote this book. The title of this book came to me one evening when I was hanging out in the pasture with Hummer.

"Horses are smart and sensitive," Ronnie said. "People treat them as if they are stupid and insensitive. We usually bring them down to our own level instead of going up to their level."

I have taken Ronnie's message to heart with my own horses and when teaching others. It's easy to stay in our comfort zone and expect our horse to change and behave in a way that makes us feel comfortable. We unknowingly do this with people all the time, too.

It is my wish that this book will inspire you to go up to the horse's level. It's possible—and each of us has felt it in our heart when we have witnessed beautiful horse-human partnerships. Often, though, we just see the results without being aware of the inner journey these people have been on to achieve such harmony with their horses.

May this book inspire you to become the best version of yourself when you interact with horses.

**"The essential joy of being with horses is that it brings us in contact with the rare elements of grace, beauty, spirit, and freedom."**

—Sharon Ralls Lemon

# My Journey

## My Beginning

Sometimes it felt like I had taken a detour in life on the way to my dream, and yet all my experiences have led me to who I am and what I can offer others.

I grew up in southern California and had wanted to work with animals from the time I was a kid. However, I ended up getting an MBA and working for large international companies for 12 years, leading and accompanying people through change processes, before horses came into my life at the age of 35. At that point I was living and working in Switzerland.

Between jobs I spent a month on a farm, offering horse therapy for handicapped children. What I observed there in the interaction between horses and humans touched me deeply. This experience became a turning point in my life, and I took the first step toward realizing my childhood dream of working with both people and animals.

I spent the next three years in jeans and cowboy boots on ranches in France and Montana (La Cense), Colorado (Parelli Center) and California (Furnace Creek Stables), living with horses and learning how they interact with people.

I loved ranch life and being outdoors with horses all day—not to mention the opportunity to work with young horses and learn from great horsemen such as Ronnie Willis and Ray Hunt, as well as from Bill and Tom Dorrance through their wonderful books. These cowboys had a tremendous impact on my approach to horses. I learned to see the world from the horse's perspective.

## My Path

After three fantastic years, I came back to Switzerland and brought with me from Montana a beautiful black Quarter Horse named Hummer.

I became a certified equine behavioral therapist to complement my hands-on experience.

Later I traveled to Bosnia-Herzegovina twice to observe and learn from the wild horses there. I was so inspired by my time with the wild horses that I used photos from those visits for my first book, *Weisheiten aus der Herde* (in German), from which I created an e-book in both German and English *(Leadership Wisdom from Horses).*

While I was still in Montana, I discovered the book *The Tao of Equus* by Linda Kohanov, a pioneer in equine-assisted learning. What I read inspired me so much that I went to Arizona in 2011 to become an Eponaquest instructor and later attended Linda's continuing education courses "Power of the Herd" and "Sentient Communication."

## Today

The Eponaquest training was another turning point in my work with people and horses. Before that, I hadn't been aware to what extent the horse's behavior reflected my own inner world—feelings, clarity, focus, insecurities, emotions, and so on.

I would correct the horse or adjust my own body language without being aware of just how much my mental and emotional state affected the horse's behavior. But once I viewed horse-human interactions from this new perspective and saw my horses as mirrors, everything changed. I learned even more about myself at much deeper levels.

It is precisely the "mirroring" that allows my coaching clients to gain powerful insights about themselves as they interact with horses. I've now integrated these aspects of self-awareness into my lessons with horse owners, with great results.

My passion is working with people and horses, with the goal of making the world a better place for horses and coaching people to reconnect and be guided by their own inner wisdom.

Horses have a unique way of helping people become the best versions of themselves. I am very grateful for my lovely horses, Hummer and Riverdance, who have been and continue to be wonderful teachers and companions in my life.

**"Every rider has that one special horse, that one horse who changes everything about them."**

—Author Unknown

# My Horses

## Hummer (Black Diamond)

At the age of 42 I bought my first horse, though I wasn't actually looking for one. A week before I headed back to Switzerland from Montana, a fellow student in the horsemanship program there said to me, "Why don't you take Hummer with you? You guys have such a great relationship!"

Well, I thought to myself, they also have horses in Switzerland, and it's a lot of stress for a five-year-old horse to leave the herd, go into quarantine for three months, fly in a plane and end up in another country, climate, etc., etc. That was my head speaking. My heart told a different story.

I had worked with a lot of young horses in Montana, but I had an especially powerful connection with Hummer. One spring morning on the ranch, I'd ridden out on Hummer with fellow students through some high grass. Unfortunately, someone had left a few metal panels on the ground, hidden by the tall spring grass. Hummer stepped on one of them, naturally got scared and starting bucking. I came off and ended up with a broken wrist—which meant no riding.

For the first four weeks I took Hummer out of the herd each day for long walks, Hummer grazing along the way. Looking back, I feel that simply spending time together with no expectations had an enormous influence on our relationship. I ended up buying Hummer, and he came to Switzerland at Easter in 2006. When my godfather first met Hummer, he nicknamed him "Black Diamond," which describes him perfectly. Hummer is the one horse that changed everything about me.

I never saw myself as a leader and just loved connecting with horses. At the same time, I realized I needed to step into this role to some extent for this horse-human partnership to work out for both of us. It's been such a rewarding journey.

I have developed on so many levels, and what I have learned from my interactions with Hummer over the years has been invaluable for working with people.

I now realize how much a horse's behavior was also a reflection of my own inner world. That was a definite game changer, and it took the partnership to another level.

For almost 10 years, I worked with Hummer for most of my riding lessons, coaching sessions and leadership workshops. Only later did I realize what it meant for a horse to deal with so many people and all the emotional baggage they unknowingly bring into their interactions with the horse.

Once I had a second horse, Hummer became semi-retired, and I stopped riding him when he turned 21. I wanted him to simply enjoy being a horse, and I wanted to say "thank you" for being my faithful companion and co-trainer over all these years. Now he only works with the coaching clients he chooses. Of course, I still do a lot with Hummer, and he is still my greatest teacher in life.

## Ribana

I adopted Ribana, together with a friend of mine, when her owner passed away. The owner's family wanted to put her down, though they had the financial resources to care for her.

I couldn't understand how they could put down a healthy horse, even an older one like Ribana, knowing how much she had given their father over a lifetime. Thankfully, a few other horse owners pitched in financially and also donated their time to help us care for Ribana. I am grateful that she could enjoy a few more wonderful years before passing on in peace and dignity when she was 28 years old.

## Riverdance

Although I had been wanting a mare for Hummer for quite a while, I'd never taken steps to make it happen. Then a dear friend of mine—someone who can sense things very well—said she saw in my future a dark brown mare with a white marking on her face. I took note of what she said and left it at that. But a week later when I was giving a workshop at a stable, there stood a horse just like the one my friend had described. I asked about the horse, and it just so happened that her owner was looking for a new home for Riverdance. That was my lucky day!

I not only loved her name, but everything about her. She wasn't in the best shape, emotionally or physically, but inside my heart I knew that things would work out fine. To this day, she is far more than I could have asked for.

Riverdance is a lovely and sensitive mare—a beautiful, tall and sleek Thoroughbred mix who requires your full attention or else she'll have other ideas about what to do with her time! Riverdance is gentle and great with kids and wonderful when working with coaching clients. And riding her is like floating over the ground. I love her princess personality.

## Saifur

I adopted Saifur and his longtime friend Redondo in 2020, both wonderful stallions and ever so polite around people. Sadly, Redondo passed away unexpectedly the same year I got him. But thankfully Saifur adapted well to his new herd and continues to do well at the age of 29.

As an Icelandic horse, summer is not his favorite time of the year. In winter he is a different horse, full of energy and quite cheeky.

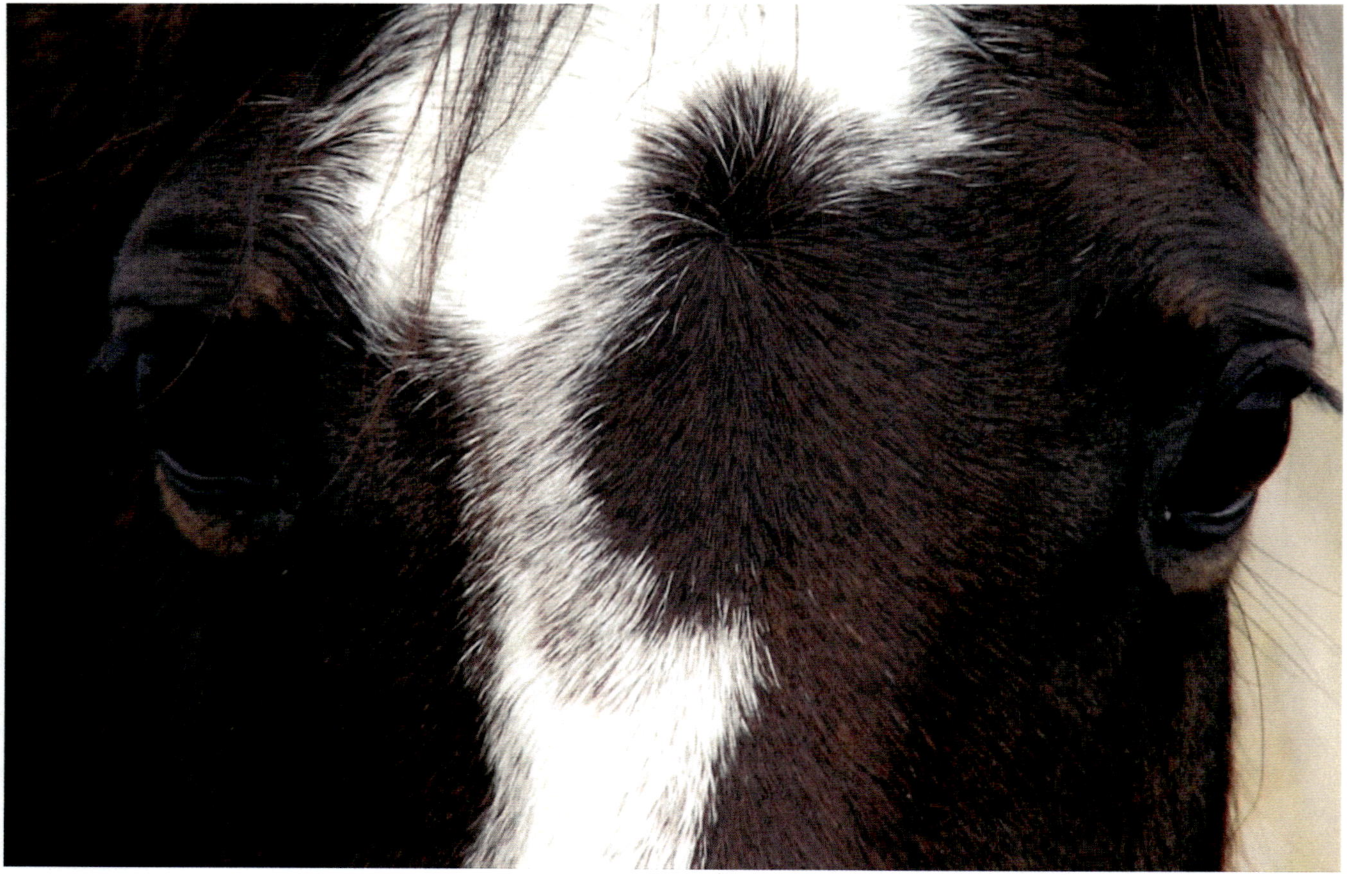

**“And I whispered to the horse, trust no man in whose eyes you do not see yourself reflected as an equal.”**

—Don Vincenzo Giobbe

# The Horse-Human Partnership

I believe we need to see and accept a horse as a sentient being in its own right, with its own opinions and ways of behaving that are unique to its species.

I also believe we should never try to change the nature of the horse, but instead explore ways of being and working together that both horse and human can feel good about and truly enjoy.

So where do you begin when you want to create a relationship that benefits both you and the horse? Creating such a partnership begins in your mind—how you see a horse. Why is this so important? The way you see and think about a horse will drive your actions, whether you are aware of it or not.

The more you see your horse as a partner, and not just a means to an end, the more effort you will put into meeting the horse's needs. Not only will physical needs be met—such as movement, good hay, fresh water—but also the emotional and mental needs, by having the horse live in a herd situation with other horses.

When you see your horse as a partner, the relationship becomes more important than any goal. In other words, you will not knowingly jeopardize the relationship just to achieve a particular goal.

Of course, when you have a happy and well-balanced horse your goals can be reached much more easily, because the horse wants to be with you. This kind of bond unleashes great potential in the horse-human partnership.

**"Give a horse what it needs and it will give you its heart in return."**

—Author Unknown

# The Needs of Horses

We tend to focus on the needs of a horse when we are with it: how do I communicate, build trust, go sideways, and more. But before you do anything at all with your horse, you need to ensure that it can live like a horse when you're not around. Why? Because a horse that is mentally, emotionally and physically balanced and feeling good will be more open and willing to do things with you. This may sound obvious, but there are still plenty of horses for whom this is not the case.

Living like a horse means just that—a stabling situation that comes as close as possible to meeting the natural needs of a horse:

**Physical.** Ideally horses live outdoors together, with access to a clean shelter that they can comfortably share. The area should provide the freedom to move in all gaits and 24/7 access to high-quality hay, grass and clean water.

Let's look at feeding in more detail. Consider the fact that horses need to eat at least 16 hours a day. Yet many have the same eating schedule as humans, meaning that they eat three times a day and then go 12 or more hours without any food. However, the horse's stomach continues to produce digestive acids in the expectation of getting food every few hours.

In the wild, horses graze up to 16 hours a day. Their stomachs are thus normally protected from ulcers due to the continuous presence of high-fiber food.

Horses have small stomachs. The stomach of a 1,000-pound horse is about as big as a football and can only hold two to five gallons of feed. That makes sense for a prey animal. This way, it is never weighed down by heavy meals and can easily flee if need be.

Hay nets are one way to extend the eating time of a horse, getting closer to the horse's natural needs for regular intake of small quantities of food.

**Emotional.** Having horses live in herds is easy in nature, where there's unlimited space. But as soon as space is limited, as in most stabling situations, the horses that live together in a herd must be carefully selected and managed.

That's why many riders naturally worry about the risk of injury in a herd setting versus keeping their horse in a stall. Ideally you'll have a herd in which no animal is stressed—meaning that the lowest-ranking horse always has easy access to food, water and a place to rest and lie down.

We can't expect a horse to fit into the herd the human has selected, though. Just because horses live in a herd, it doesn't mean they will naturally get along—just as we may come across people at work that we don't particularly like. I know of one horse that lives in a herd but is a loner because it's just not a good fit.

Ideally the herd is also a situation in which there's not much change. Having horses leave and introducing new ones stresses the entire herd every time. Just think about how good it feels to come home to a place where you feel comfortable and relaxed. It's no different for your horse.

**Mental.** A herd life is good for the mind, too. It keeps horses alert and interacting with their surroundings.

## Nature of the Horse

Every horse has these instinctual needs, and they haven't changed since horses were domesticated more than 5,000 years ago. If these innate needs aren't met, the result can be behavioral issues in the short run and health issues in the long run.

I've seen horses chew wood as a displaced behavior, weave in their box, or become hard to handle because they have no outlet for their built-up energy.

A horse's needs must also be a top priority in breeding and training. It's quite sad that most horses never get to know their fathers. And foals are taken away from their moms too early—usually abruptly, from one day to the next, leaving emotional scars in both the foal and its mother.

In nature, a foal remains close to its mother until about 8 to 10 months of age, before the next foal is born. Even then, the yearling remains with its extended family.

While training, you must consider the natural development of a horse, both physically and mentally. A horse can be considered physically ready around the age of six when all the bones have properly fused together. A horse can be considered mentally ready at about the same time as reflected in its ability to concentrate and deal with new situations. This means that considerable care must be taken with anything we do before that age. At the same time, we must recognize that some horses will not be ready to start work or be trained when we think they should be or when we want them to be.

When proper attention is given to the horse's needs early on and throughout its life, a healthy horse can easily live to be 30 or more years old.

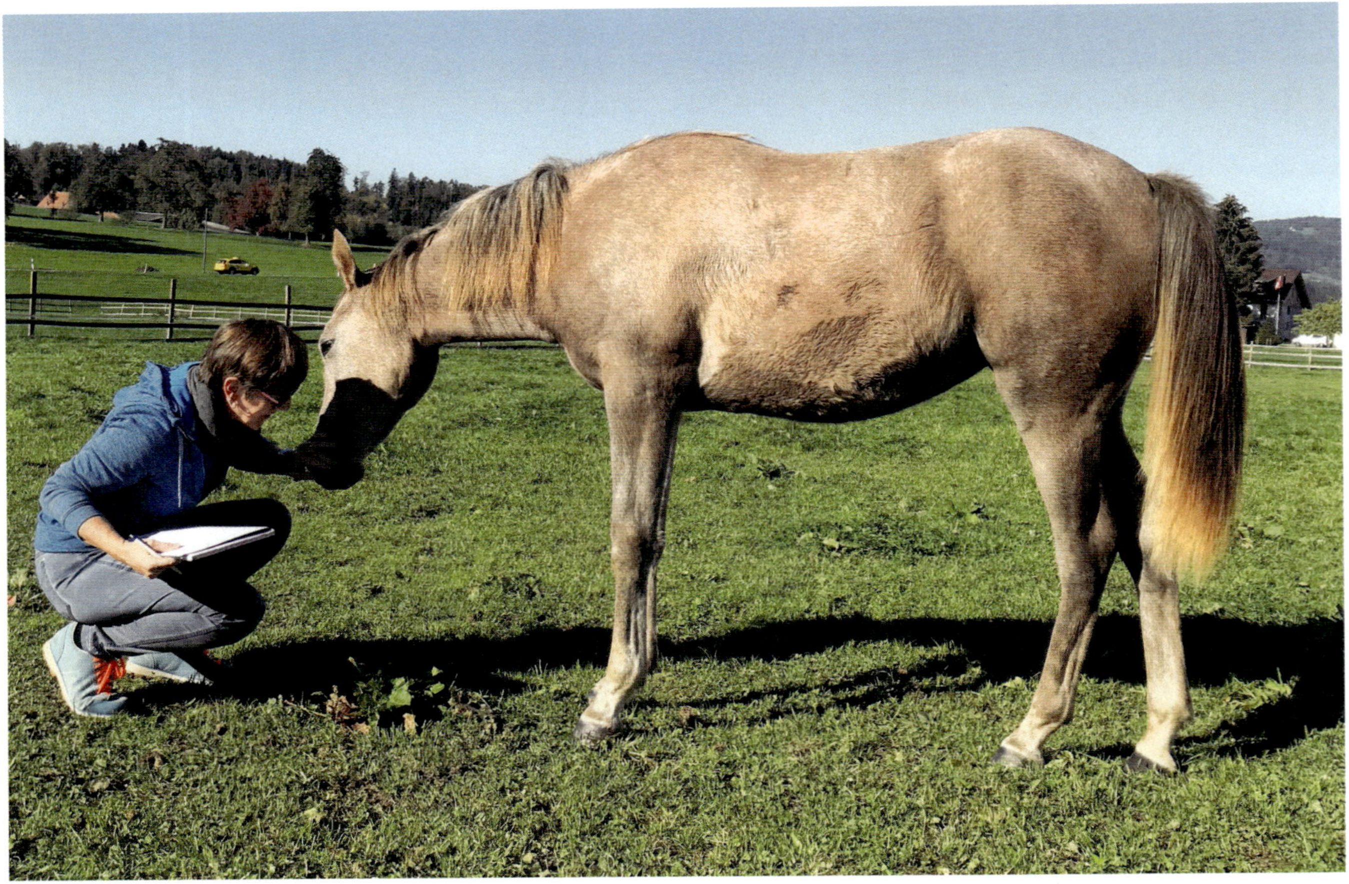

**"It is only with the heart that one sees rightly; what is essential is invisible to the eye."**

—Antoine de Saint-Exupéry

# You and Your Horse

As a starting point, it's good to be aware of a few things regarding the horse-human relationship. Here are three questions to head us in that direction. Take a few moments to reflect on each one and write down your thoughts.

- Why do you have or want a horse?
- What's in it for you?
- What's in it for the horse?

## Why do you have or want a horse?

Many people dream of having a horse. It's easy to understand why. Horses are such elegant and majestic creatures that they draw us to them in unexplainable ways. One woman who had heard about my horse Riverdance through a mutual friend then dreamed about her, and one day she came out to the stables to spend time and ride with her. I am happy to share my love for horses with other people!

After I'd spent three years of learning from and with horses, I was ready to have my own horse to explore the potential of the horse-human relationship. That is when I got Hummer, back in 2006. Thanks to Hummer and 20 years of interacting with horses, I realize that I have become a different person. Horses have been and continue to be the best teachers in my life. It's so beautiful to experience the magic moments when love and trust are the common language.

If you are thinking about getting a horse, please consider where the horse is at and where you are right now—mentally, emotionally and physically. What grade are you in? What grade is your horse in? Be honest in your evaluation. If the gap is too wide, consider walking away. Or ask yourself if you are truly willing to do what it takes to meet the horse where it's at and to give yourself and/or the horse the time to come together.

Do you already have a horse? Take a moment and write down why you have a horse and what you love most about your horse.

## What's in it for you?

For me, having horses has been an incredible opportunity to grow as a person. My horses are often my mirrors. Based on their reactions, I see what is really going on inside of myself. I love the fact that I can spend hours with them without ever saying a word—truly a beautiful form of connection and interaction.

We get a lot from horses in so many ways. A friend of mine once said, "I give my psychologist hay and water," referring to the many times she could just go spend time with her horse when life became challenging. I, too, have been thankful to be able to just hang with horses when I was feeling down.

We not only receive a lot but must also give a lot to have a horse. We give our time and money to have a horse, and that amounts to quite a lot over the lifetime of a horse. But I don't regret a single moment or penny that I've spent on my horse.

What's in it for you to have a horse?

## What's in it for the horse?

This question is something we rarely think about, but it's very important to answer if we are to consider the horse's point of view. What can you offer your horse in this relationship?

Below are some questions on which to reflect. Write down your answers and then, taking everything into consideration, ask yourself if you would want to *be* your horse.

**Physically**

- What kind of "feel" can you offer your horse?
- Are you in good physical shape?
- How well will the horse's needs be looked after?

**Emotionally**

- What qualities can you offer your horse as a friend, partner, and leader?
- How is your emotional fitness level?

**Mentally**

- Are you willing to look at a situation through your horse's eyes?
- Are you willing to reflect upon and change your way of seeing your horse?

**“You are not working on the horse; you are working on yourself.”**

—Ray Hunt

# Your Journey

This book is meant to guide you on your own personal journey toward becoming the friend and leader your horse needs you to be. It consists of a collection of topics that have been very helpful on my journey with horses.

As Ronnie Willis said, "Horses are like snowflakes, no two are alike," so let yourself be inspired by this book and use whatever fits your personal situation.

I would not be who I am today without horses. Their honest feedback to whatever I was thinking, feeling, or doing has helped me notice what was going on inside of me and how this affected others. If I wanted different results, I had to work on myself and not on the horse. So often we try to change the outside world—a situation with our horse, our friends, our family, our boss—not realizing that the outside world is often a mirror of our inside world and is there to help us grow, especially in challenging situations.

How often do we correct a horse that resists what we are offering without first becoming aware of our own mental and emotional states or behavior? Without this self-awareness, we try to change the horse's behavior instead of taking a moment to reflect on our own behavior and what we are thinking or feeling. Self-awareness is one of the biggest things I learned from interacting with horses and it has helped me in so many ways in relationships and when collaborating with others.

Take the time to reflect on each topic. You will come across blank pages at the end of some sections. This is intentional. Life is often so busy that we go from A to B to C to Z and consume information all day long without ever taking a breather. We don't take the time to reflect on our experiences and consciously integrate them into our life. If we discover free time on our agenda, we always have the feeling we have to fill this space, when in fact this space can serve as an important reminder to "take a break, to stop and smell the roses."

Being open to learning from horses and listening to what they have to share with you, and your journey will open doors to beautiful and magical experiences in the horse-human partnership.

**“If you get ahead of him, it is just tolerance and not acceptance. If push comes to shove, he will take over instead of filling in for you.”**

—Ronnie Willis

## Acceptance

So how can you tell when your horse accepts or approves of what you are doing? Acceptance takes place in the horse's mind and is reflected in its body. Its body will be relaxed and its eyes soft. Your horse will move smoothly and feel good to you. It's like having a good dance partner.

The difference between acceptance and tolerance is quite easy to see when horses are being groomed or have to stand still and wait a few minutes. I have seen so many horses that just tolerate grooming, because if they resist they get in trouble with the rider.

If a horse is talking to you and you don't listen, it makes it hard for a horse to truly accept you. Maybe it's just trying to tell you that a certain brush or the way you are grooming doesn't feel good.

We can also see the difference between acceptance and tolerance when teaching a horse to stand still and wait. Stopping usually isn't the problem, but waiting is. Just because a horse is standing still physically doesn't mean it means it's standing still mentally, in its head. You can easily see this in its body language; the horse is tense, its head is up, and it's looking around. In this state, the horse is more or less tolerating the situation and is usually just waiting for you not to pay attention for a moment so it can walk off and move its feet.

It may take a few repetitions of teaching the horse to wait until you say it's okay to walk off. If a horse who is still in the learning process is nervous, you need to wait for the one second when it focuses on you and then walk off together with the horse.

Always keep in mind what behavior you desire. If you'd like the horse to check in with you to see if it's okay to walk off, then you want to reward this behavior. Should it walk off without checking in, don't give in just because it's easier to do so. Stop the horse and wait for it to relax and focus on you, and then walk off together.

When horses are tense while being groomed, led, or ridden, or simply when they are in the presence of people, often they are just tolerating the interaction with the human. It's the same as when you may just be tolerating your boss at work; you'd rather work for someone else, but you simply have to deal with the situation until you can change things. It's the same for horses. There will always be situations that both horses and people have to put up with, but these should be the exceptions and not the rule.

The most common sign of tolerance is when a horse swishes its tail. The horse is saying, "Okay, I'll do it, but something about your asking is not okay with me." Maybe your timing was off, or you were unbalanced or unclear.

It's important to note that when a horse is merely tolerating a person, it's difficult for it to focus on much else because of the inner resistance toward what it's being asked to do. You want to have a horse in an open frame of mind, willing to listen to what you're asking it to do.

Just as important as your horse accepting you as a friend, leader, and rider, you want to make sure it also accepts the saddle (its placement, type of cinch), the bit (how it's worn and used as a form of communication) and any aids you use, such as a crop. It must never be afraid of any aid. I've seen horses move away as soon as someone lifted a crop—not a good sign. This often indicates the horse associates the crop with an unpleasant experience. Ideally, the crop is merely seen an extension of your arm by your horse. This means you can stroke the horse all over its body with the crop as you could with your hand.

To move from tolerance to acceptance, you need to be aware of how and what you are doing and present things in a way that is suitable to the horse.

Like a great dancer, everything must be done with feel and be fine-tuned based on the horse's reaction. When something feels good to your horse, it will enjoy the time with you; otherwise, it will prefer to be back at the stable with the other horses.

**"When we show our respect for other living things, they respond with respect for us."**

—Arapaho

# Approach

In the hustle and bustle of everyday life, we often get to the barn, eager to see our horse, and walk toward it with halter in hand, ready to do something. In doing so, we forget to ask permission to enter the horse's space and are surprised when it walks away instead of toward us. If we had slowed down, mentally and physically, taken the time to observe its body language and changed our approach accordingly, then the horse would have had no reason to walk away.

Here's how you can approach your horse in a way that builds curiosity and often will draw your horse toward you. I learned this from Linda Kohanov. Mindfully approaching your horse means noticing when your horse's body language changes in response to your presence and responding accordingly.

Body language changes in your horse will be ear movements and posture shifts resulting from a mild increase in stress as the horse's autonomic nervous system notices there's something new in the environment, in this case a human walking over to it. This is called a "proximity response."

When you see this proximity response and learn to respond accordingly with a "rock back and sigh," it will naturally draw your horse to you. From a polyvagal informed perspective, the rock back and sigh stimulates the ventral vagal complex in mammals that encourages relaxation and social connection.

Unrestrained horses will walk away from people who are holding their breath, and are attracted to people as they audibly exhale with a long, relaxed outbreath.

Here is how you can use this approach with your horse, whether it's in the box, outdoor paddock, or on the pasture. First center yourself with even inbreaths and outbreaths before walking toward your horse. Then as you walk toward it and notice a proximity response, then stop, rock back and sigh by putting the weight on your back foot, dropping your shoulders and exhaling with a long, relaxed outbreath and then continuing with long even inbreaths and outbreaths. Wait until your horse relaxes before continuing to move toward it. Again, when you note the next proximity response, stop, put your weight on your back foot, drop your shoulders take a long, relaxed outbreath and continue breathing even inbreaths and outbreaths. In doing so, you are being respectful of the horse's space by asking permission before you proceed.

At about the third proximity response you will be about 4 1/2 feet away and on the perimeter of your horse's personal space. In my experience, most horses will come to you at this point after you rock back and sigh. If not, and the horse is standing still, then you have permission to enter its personal space.

You can rub on your horse's favorite spots before putting the halter on—a way to reward the horse for standing still before leading it away from the other horses.

Here, too, observe the horse's response as you start to pet or rub on it. Your horse may not necessarily want to be petted every time it comes up to you. If the head moves away or the ears go back, stop immediately and respect your horse's response.

Remember that the stable, whether it's a box or an open pen, is a horse's bedroom. Be careful not to invade, and instead ask to be welcomed in.

And keep in mind that the size of your horse's bubble can vary. People are no different; sometimes we love the company of others, while on other days we need more space.

Every so often I have days when I approach Hummer and he walks away. Then I approach again, and if I get the same response, I walk away. Sometimes this happens when I'm stressed. My mind is going a mile a minute and I unknowingly hold my breath or take short inbreaths and outbreaths. Although I "think" I'm relaxed and go through the motions of approaching Hummer, he senses how I'm really doing from a mile away and essentially says, "No, thanks."

On other days, the same response from Hummer or Riverdance might simply mean, "I'd rather stay out in the pasture today." That's fine with me, and I will respect this.

If your horse always walks away when you arrive and only comes when you bribe it with carrots or apples, then maybe you need to rethink how to spend time with your horse, from the horse's perspective.

Is being with the human enough of a reason to leave the herd? What's in it for the horse when it spends time with you, other than a chance to get some exercise?

Even when horses come to us, sometimes they just want to say hello and hang out with us, but then quickly move away when we want to stroke them. We have to learn to respect a horse that doesn't want to be touched.

There are days when my horses love to be stroked and brushed, and other days when they don't want that at all. At first I took this personally, but now I realize that my horses are simply expressing their needs, no more and no less.

"True horsemanship is developed in the mindful quality of everything we do, not just in the quality of everything we do with our horses."

—Mark Rashid

## Attitude

Your attitude determines your behavior. Is it all about "me" or all about "we"? If it's all about "me," eventually you will run into problems with your horse in terms of unwanted behaviors and possibly even health issues.

A "me" attitude shows up when the horse is a means to an end. A "we" attitude, on the other hand, shows up when you are looking for a true lifelong partner—when you are open to the horse's opinion and allow it to influence your behavior.

This "me" or "we" is already in play when you decide to buy a horse. What's in it for the horse? What can you offer the horse?

Your attitude determines the quality of each interaction with your horse. With a positive attitude, you'll see the best in your horse, even in difficult situations. You will always be able to recognize that your horse is trying.

I remember coming back from a trail ride with a friend when it had started raining. In pouring rain, we had to unsaddle and load the horses into the trailer. Thankfully, Hummer went in quickly. The other horse didn't see the need to go in yet, despite the rain, so my friend had gone from a positive to a negative attitude—understandably, as we were getting more and more soaked. My ability to remain positive and calm helped the situation. You always need to reflect on whether you are part of the problem or part of the solution, even if you aren't directly involved.

It's also important to recognize the horse's attitude toward doing something and to reward its effort or positive attitude, such as ears forward. Noticing and responding to such slight changes can go a long way in your relationship with your horse.

**“Horses are our mirrors. They can be in balance when we are in balance.”**

—Marijke de Jong

## Balance

Balance is essential to the health and well-being of both people and animals. We see balance everywhere in nature; in day and night, the seasons, tidal ebb and flow. Wild horses instinctively seek a balance between eating, playing and resting. Horses in the care of humans also need a balanced life.

When you look at how you spend time with your horse, what is the balance between giving and taking, between doing something and doing nothing, between being gentle and being firm, between playing and working, between movement and rest, between learning and repetition, between riding on a loose or collected rein, between arena work and trail riding?

Take the time to reflect and see what areas are in balance and what areas are out of balance with your horse at the moment.

If you are unsure of any area, take a closer look at your horse's behavior. If you spend too much time in the arena and too little time trail riding, your horse may become demotivated and drag its feet as you walk toward the arena.

Anything that stays out of balance for too long, if not addressed, will cause both physiological and physical problems. Just think of how many sports horses are "retired" or in horse heaven because they were pushed too early and too long in a single direction, well beyond their mental and physical limits. School horses can also "burn out" because they only see the inside of an arena and deal with beginners all day long.

To help balance things, it would be good to have school horses do groundwork with experienced riders or be ridden by them so they are mentally and physically challenged on a regular basis.

Balance plays such an important role in the quality of life. Think about your own life for a moment. The areas that feel good to you will most likely be those that are in balance.

Balance is essential to riding. A horse that is out of balance can get worried and start going faster when the rider is also out of balance. This is an attempt to regain its own balance. That is why an independent seat, where you don't need your reins and legs for balance, has such a big influence on how a horse feels when ridden. In addition, a rider with an independent and thus more relaxed seat can more easily follow the movement of the horse at all gaits.

We also cause a horse to get out of balance by not properly preparing it for transitions. This means it doesn't have time to rearrange itself beforehand. You see this often in downward transitions when the horse's head goes up; raising its head is an effort to put its weight on the hindquarters to regain balance. Horses can be prepared for upward and downward transitions with energetic cues such as deep inward or outward breaths.

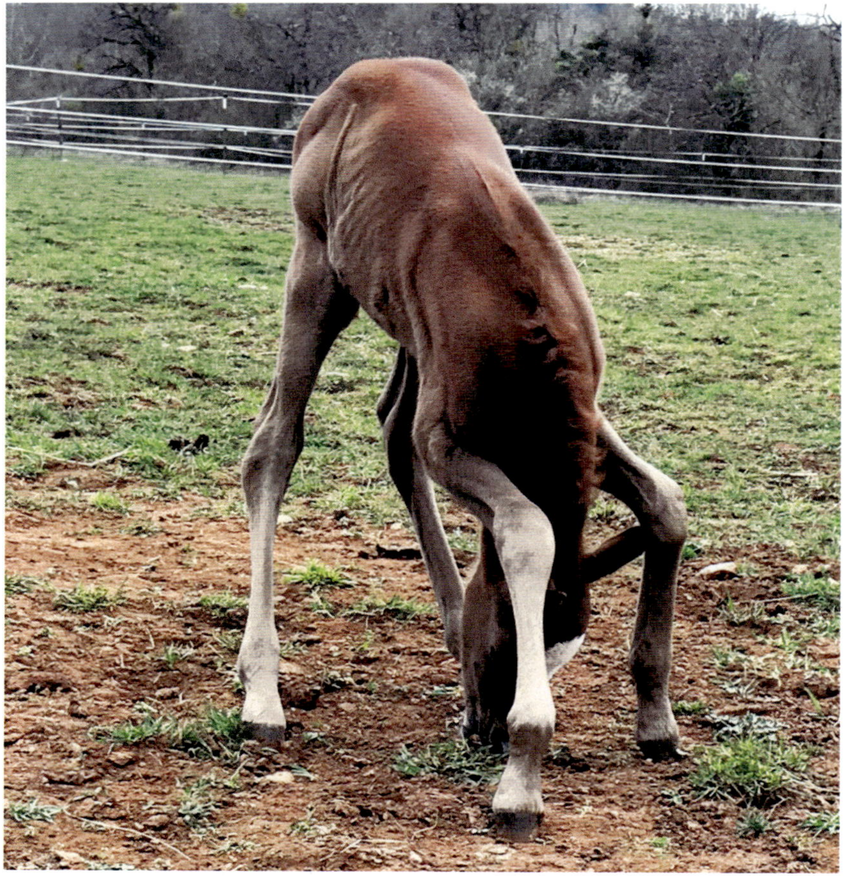

**“Believe in your horse, so your horse can believe in you.”**

—Ray Hunt

## Belief

I believed in my horses from day one, not knowing what we were going to do or experience together. Believing in myself was more of a challenge.

I realized this with Riverdance, who as a Thoroughbred mix was quite a contrast to my Quarter Horse, Hummer. My goal was to ride her in the forest without a bit at all three gaits, as I did with Hummer. I knew she could do it, but it took me about three years to get there.

The process took me well outside my comfort zone, but I worked at it little by little and eventually made it. I had to put aside my ego—which had the tendency to compare myself with riders who could have done it in much less time—and stay focused on just myself. The only person with whom I needed to compare myself was me.

We have to be careful not to let our own beliefs and fears limit what we or our horses can do. Many people won't inconvenience themselves to get outside of their comfort zone and address the fears that hold them back from what they want to achieve, in life and with their horse.

What you and your horse can and will achieve is directly related to what you believe is possible. Your horse can feel whether or not you believe in it.

Believing in your horse changes the way you interact with it. You have patience because you know you'll get to your goal together. When your horse is bothered by one way of doing something, you look for another way.

**"When you own your breath, no one can steal your peace."**

—Author Unknown

## Breath

Breath is life. Breath is energy. And energy is the language of life. How you're breathing in this moment as you read this text is subconsciously telling your body how you're responding to the outside world. Many chemical processes take place as a result of your breathing without your ever knowing it. But breathing can be used consciously, too, to change how you respond to the outside world.

When you are stressed, your body automatically switches to the fight-or-flight mode. Your breathing becomes shallow, your blood pressure increases, your adrenaline increases and you can't think clearly—not ideal when you are supposed to be the leader for your horse.

The solution is simple: change your breathing. Consciously begin taking deep breaths in through your nose, counting from 1 to 5, and breathe deeply out through your mouth, counting backward from 5 to 1. This will shift your body from the fight-or-flight mode to a relaxation and recovery mode. You'll be in a frame of mind to think clearly again.

At first when I was trail riding with Riverdance and she saw or heard something unexpected, she'd stop dead in her tracks. I'd also get nervous and wonder what all the fuss was about. I'd tense up, shorten my reins and talk with her to say that all was well, but this changed little, because my short and shallow breathing was communicating another message—that I, too, was worried. I usually waited until Riverdance calmed down so that I could calm down as well. However, that made me dependent on her, and as her leader I needed to let Riverdance know that all was well—not the other way around.

One of the easiest ways I found to do this was to change how I was breathing—to go from shallow (4 seconds for an in-and-out breath) to deep breathing (10 seconds for each in-and-out breath). This not only calmed me down and gave me mental clarity about what to do next, but it also communicated to Riverdance that she could relax. I've found this to be extremely effective—that I could simply use my breathing to co-regulate another being. This is especially useful when this other being is a 1,000-pound prey animal whose natural instinct is to leave right away and ask questions later.

**"If it feels good to a horse, it will do it again. If it does not feel good to a horse, it will not do it again."**

—Ronnie Willis

## Comfort

Why is it important that a horse feels comfortable? When your horse is comfortable, you will have its full attention, and it can more easily carry out what you are asking because it's not distracted. Whenever a saddle doesn't fit properly, a horse will try to compensate by moving differently to avoid the discomfort.

We don't buy, let alone wear, shoes or clothes for ourselves that are uncomfortable. Yet so many horses have saddles, saddle pads, girths, bits, or horse boots that don't fit properly.

If you find that your horse's behavior has changed for no apparent reason, always check both your equipment and your horse's health. Problems with teeth, for example, not only influence the way horses eat but also the way they carry the bit or move their hindquarters.

Investing in the horse's comfort and well-being must be a top priority. Otherwise you will spend money on vets and therapists to correct the physical damage that has been done over the years—not to mention the fact that it's simply unfair to the horse.

A rider can be a source of discomfort to the horse, as well. Riders who don't have a good seat and then pull on the reins or hold on with their legs for balance are a constant source of irritation to the horse. And riders not only affect their horse physically but also mentally and emotionally when they aren't emotionally balanced or they have a negative attitude. How would you like to be around someone like that?

We can work with both comfort and discomfort when teaching a horse. Once I had a horse who was very eager to get back to the barn. Ronnie Willis always said, "Don't make the wrong thing impossible for the horse, just uncomfortable."

So instead of using the reins to stop my horse from walking at a too-fast pace toward the barn, I simply turned it around 180 degrees and we backed up in the direction of the barn. When I felt the horse was tired of walking backward, we turned around, but as soon as it started picking up the pace, we went backward again. The horse naturally preferred a forward motion, and after a few repetitions, going backward was uncomfortable enough that we walked to the barn at a normal pace.

A friend of mine had a similar problem. When her horse trotted to the stables, she didn't stop it but simply insisted that it trot past the stables. After trotting past a few times, that also became too uncomfortable for the horse. As its goal was to get home, it finally walked to the stables at a normal pace.

"Yes" and "no" is how people think. But basically, if something feels good to a horse, it will do it again. If it does not feel good to a horse, it will not do it again.

**"It is easy to get along with a horse if you think like a horse."**

—Ronnie Willis

# Communication

Communication is a huge topic and much has already been said about it over the years. In this section, you will come across factors that influence communication, but that may not be so obvious at first because they happen unconsciously.

One such factor is your heart. It's one of the most important, yet often overlooked factors, in effective communication. Little do most people know, for example, that the heart's electromagnetic field broadcasts a much stronger signal to the world than that of the brain. The heart's magnetic field, which contains your emotions, is 5'000x stronger than that of your brain and its electrical field is 50x stronger. This explains why horses respond more to how you are feeling in your heart and less to what you are thinking in your head. You cannot think I am not scared and pretend to act in this way, when in fact you feel scared inside. The horse will respond to how you feel and not how you act.

The following are some of the other key factors to communicating effectively, with the least amount of effort, with your horse.

## Clarity

**"The horse is interested in clarity and sureness."**

—Leslie Desmond

You need to be 90 to 100 percent sure about what you want and how you are going to get there *before* communicating with your horse. This goes along the lines of 80 percent preparation and 20 percent implementation.

Let's say you want to weave in and out of a row of cones. As you are wondering if you should come from the right or the left and in the last moment decide to come from the left, although the horse is headed to the right, you will need to correct it to get back to where you want to be. If you had been clear about what you wanted from the beginning, this extra effort could have been avoided.

Why should a horse follow someone who doesn't know what they want or where they are going? It can be a waste of energy from the horse's perspective. On the other hand, if you are clear about what you want, then you can be a lighthouse for your horse, a source of orientation.

## Congruence

**"The horse shows us when we are acting from our authentic self. When we resonate from this place, the horse feels safe and acts accordingly."**

—Sara Fancy

The way we communicate often confuses horses, because our actions aren't in alignment with the way we truly feel. Horses are just the opposite. Their actions are always in alignment with how they feel. This explains why horses communicate so effectively. The biggest challenge for people is to attain this level of congruence in their own communication. Thankfully, horses give us immediate and honest feedback to let us know how we are doing.

Why don't we act on the outside the way we feel on the inside? Maybe we were taught early on to hide the way we truly feel. As children, we may have learned that hiding our true feelings allowed us to be more easily accepted and loved by our parents, and we unknowingly carried this behavior into adult life.

Even society encourages conformity over authenticity. Only when I began working with horses did I really became aware of this incongruence—what it meant in my own life and how it influenced my communication with others. So often in my leadership training for companies, people are nervous if not outright scared about working with our 1,000-pound co-trainers. Of course, only a few admit this at the beginning of a workshop when they first come in contact with the horse.

But since the focus is on leading through connection and trust, the first thing participants learn is to have the courage to express their genuine emotions. As soon as this happens, the horse will walk up to them. Why? Because the person is no longer wearing a mask and pretending not to be nervous. This builds trust.

People are always surprised and wonder how horses can notice such a subtle change from a distance. They are simply picking up on the quality of the energy someone is broadcasting, and whether it's clear or muddled. That's the beauty of interacting with such highly sensitive beings; people become of aware of what is going on inside of themselves, and the impact it has on others.

Congruence builds trust. Horses that aren't confident and naturally look for a leader in the human can become even more insecure when they interact with people who are incongruent—i.e., wearing a mask.

## Heart

**"Your energy introduces you before you even speak."**
—Author Unknown

We communicate more information than we ever realize when we interact with horses. So many times I have seen someone wanting to stop an approaching horse. They can get pretty loud, yet something about them is inviting the horse to walk all over them. This "something" is what the person is feeling—in this case, uncertainty.

A horse will always respond to how people feel in their hearts. This is the energy that is being broadcast, and it's what a horse picks up on and responds to.

My horse Hummer is always looking for an authentic connection from the heart and can pick up on how I'm feeling from quite a distance. The days when I think I should do something with him but don't feel it in my heart often are the days when he doesn't come to me. I respect his response and don't insist that he come, or go to get him. Sometimes I may just hang out in the pasture or say hello and then go off to do something else.

When we try to hide how we really feel—as we do around other people all the time—it makes communication with the horse even more difficult. You can think, "I'm not scared," but if you actually feel scared inside, your horse will know it.

Deliberately suppressing an emotion takes part of the focus away from what you are doing with the horse. This can bother a horse in two ways. First, you are not fully present as a leader. Second, you are being incongruent; you are not acting based on how you feel. This can cause a horse to not trust you.

Energy—not words or body language—is the universal language. Words and body language influence how we feel, and how we feel is contained in the energy our heart sends out to the world.

## Listening

**"If you listen to your horse with more than your two ears, you will hear it talking with you."**

—Author Unknown

Your horse is talking to you all the time. The question is, how often are you really listening? The goal of listening to your horse is to figure out what it understands and what it doesn't, what bothers it and what doesn't.

Let's say you are trotting along, and whenever you go back down to a walk the horse's head pops up. Now you look for what's bothering your horse during the downward transition. When you listen to your horse, you may discover the link between what you just did and how your horse responded. I've seen how a simple change in the asking has resulted in a smooth transition, with almost no extra effort.

If you get stuck at any time with your horse, slow things down and really focus on the horse and what it's trying to communicate to you with its behavior. Look at the situation from the horse's perspective and you should find the answer there. This means letting go of everything you are thinking about a situation and being open to what you sense and feel. What is your gut feeling or intuition telling you when you open your heart and listen to your horse? Be honest with yourself. Maybe you didn't do something you should have done. Nobody is expecting you to be perfect. Just acknowledge the situation and move on.

If you want a horse to listen to you more when you are doing groundwork or riding, try giving it more responsibility.

If you are used to controlling every single movement, the horse becomes like a robot with no need to think for itself. But once you can let go of your need to control and get to where you can trust the horse more, you can give it more and more responsibility. A great way to do this is by riding on a looser rein. The horse then has to focus more on you to figure out what you want. It becomes a mental game for the horse, and the more mental effort a horse puts in, the more physical effort he will put in. In the end, it becomes easier for you and more interesting for the horse.

## Silence

**"Silence isn't empty. It's full of answers."**

—Author Unknown

One thing I love most about being around horses is that I can spend hours with them doing different things and not a word is spoken, yet we are constantly communicating with one another.

Experiment with being silent. Do what you usually do with your horse, but don't talk while you're doing it. Start slowly and just be quiet when you go to get your horse, or try it while grooming. Soon things will become quiet in your head and you'll pay much more attention to your horse, and you may notice things you might not have noticed before. You may even pay more attention to your own body language and what you are communicating to your horse.

Being silent basically allows you to more easily focus on the conversation you are having with your horse.

## Understanding

**"What I know about the horse,
I learned from the horse."**

—Tom Dorrance

You must seek to understand the nature of the horse, as this determines how to interact with horses in a way that makes sense to them. Try speaking English in a foreign country and expecting people to understand you. That simply doesn't work, to say nothing about cultural differences and ways of thinking. It's no different with a horse. You need to do what it takes to understand them.

Remember, horses aren't looking to be with humans. We made a choice to have them be a part of our lives. Therefore, it's our responsibility to try to understand everything about them—how they think, how they act, what's important to them—and communicate in a way that makes sense to them.

## Visualization

**"Visualize your success, then take action."**

—Author Unknown

This is an important key to achieving your goals. Professional athletes use visualization all the time. They rehearse the perfect wave, the perfect serve, the perfect jump over and over again in their mind, in as much detail as possible. As with most things in life, it's 80 percent preparation and 20 percent implementation.

Mental preparation is definitely more important than physical preparation and can be a game changer in the results you get.

Since the universal language is energy, why not use visualization with your horse? Many studies have shown that the part of your brain that gets activated by thinking about an action is the same part of the brain that gets activated when you are actually doing the action.

Because of my own experience with animal communication, mentally receiving pictures from animals, I also believe that horses can in some way pick up on the images we are sending them.

Before doing an exercise with your horse, *visualize the desired goal as if it is has already happened.* Then adding the feeling of having achieved your goal to the visualisation will generate a positive energy that the horse will pick up on, enabling both of you to begin the exercise with a good feeling inside.

What should you do when you've visualized things and it still doesn't work? Take a moment and ask yourself these questions: Did I give my horse enough time? Could I have been clearer? Look at it from the horse's perspective to find out what you need to change.

In the section ahead on Focus, a situation is described in which a rider is being asked to visualize herself riding in front of Queen Elizabeth. That's just one example of how visualization helps you achieve a goal.

Another client had a horse that always spooked at a certain point on a trail, whether she was leading it or riding it. I took her horse and told her I didn't want to know where this problem point was. The horse didn't spook when I led it on the same trail because I had no mental image of it spooking at a given point on the trail. I was not stressed and therefore my body never tensed up nor did my blood pressure increase, both of which a horse will mirror due to the contagious nature of body sensations and emotions.

To help you better deal with stressful situations in general, learn how to breathe into the tension, follow this by an even longer outbreath to activate the parasympathetic nervous system enabling you to better focus and enter into a problem-solving mindset.

**"A bird sitting on a tree is never afraid of the branch breaking because her trust is not in the branch, but her own wings."**

—Author Unknown

## Confidence

Horses, like children, are born confident. It's the way we treat them as they grow up that either builds or takes away from their innate confidence.

It has always been my goal to have confident horses that feel good about themselves. Of course, having a pair of confident horses can be a handful when they both have the same idea and I have a different one!

I've experienced this quite a few times with Hummer and Riverdance. They both want to go one way, and I want to go the other way. Sometimes I go with my idea, sometimes theirs.

Whenever you come across a new situation for your horse, you want to present it in a way that builds confidence. Say you have to cross over a new bridge, and the horse is pretty nervous. It's obviously much easier for a horse if you get off and lead it from the ground, because then you are out in front. Crossing with you in the saddle is more challenging for the horse, since it's now the one out in front. Whether you get off and lead or stay in the saddle can also be a question of where you can be the better leader for your horse.

When I was a less confident rider, I got off more frequently. Now that I can handle more as a rider, I get off less often but am able to offer the horse the same level of guidance and confidence.

Unfamiliar situations help you to see where the confidence of the rider and horse stand. It's how you deal with these situations that either builds or takes away a horse's confidence—not to mention its trust in the rider.

I remember when I brought Hummer from Montana to Switzerland. He had never before seen a stroller, kids playing soccer, or people flying motorized planes. I simply continued exposing him to such new situations at his own pace (learning zone) without ever over-exposing him (panic zone), as that would have affected the trust he had in me as a leader.

With Hummer, I was confident in most everything we did together. Hummer was rock solid and not fazed by much. Even when I was unsure, he was fine.

When Riverdance came into my life, I had to get out of my comfort zone to be as confident with her as

I was with Hummer. My confidence grew with each day that I spent with Riverdance, and after a while I knew I could deal with most issues that came up. That confidence came through in my body language. I walked differently when leading her and sat differently in the saddle, and my posture and breathing became more relaxed. I know that Riverdance picked up on these changes, letting her trust me even more.

Losing confidence in your horse is something that needs to be addressed right away. When your horse's behavior bothers you, it will influence and later determine what you do or don't do with the horse.

I heard of a woman who only rides in the indoor arena because she is too frightened to ride outdoors. Remember—it's never too late to ask for help so that you can regain your confidence.

I lost some self-confidence when I lost control of Riverdance one day in an open area and she kept going faster and faster. The next time I went on that trail I was apprehensive and really had to focus on my breathing to stay relaxed and create a mental image of us trotting in a relaxed manner. It took me a bit of courage, but I kept her at a trot even though she definitely wanted to canter. At first it was a struggle, but after two or three tries she got the message and we trotted the whole stretch. I had to repeat this a few times to anchor it in for both of us. It's all about learning and growing together.

**“Technique can get you to a certain level.**
**But beyond that, a certain connection with the horse’s heart is necessary.”**

—Nuno Oliveira

## Connection

When I wish to connect with horses, I first need to be present, centered and connected to myself. I've noticed that this state draws horses to me, and not just my own. Basically it's an energetic feel I'm offering, like an invitation to connect, and horses respond very well. I believe this is because it's part of their natural state.

Connection can appear elusive at first, because it's simply something you *feel*. If you connect with your horse, both of you know it; and if you don't, you also both know it.

When you watch a mare lick her foal, you can feel the connection between the two, and it's heartwarming to observe this. If you've ever watched a herd of horses moving together, it seems as if there's an invisible something connecting them as they move as one over the open terrain.

I believe connection begins in our hearts. You must have a willingness to connect with your horse. It's like an invitation for your horse. If it accepts your offer, this already means a lot. Let's say you go out to get your horse from the pasture. You could walk up, put on the halter and walk off without ever connecting. Or you could attempt to connect by bringing your attention into your heart while looking at your horse from a distance. Then, as it looks up and sees you, your heart opens up even more because you are connecting with a dear friend. It's ideal to have this connection from the beginning, before you actually do something with your horse. On some days it will take longer, because your mind is busy thinking and your attention isn't on the horse. You always need to connect with yourself first before you can connect with your horse, because true connection happens via your heart.

Grooming is a great opportunity to practice connection. Instead of seeing grooming as something that has to be done before you ride, try changing your perspective and seeing it as a chance to connect with your horse.

Use deep breathing—five seconds for the in-breath through your nose and five seconds for the out-breath through your mouth—to bring you into the present moment. You will find that your movements become smoother and less rushed.

One client who used deep breathing to connect with her horse while grooming noticed that the horse started turning its head to look back at her every so often. Normally it had just stared straight ahead. As she connected with her horse, it connected with her.

The present is where your horse spends all of its time. To stay connected, at least one part of you must stay focused on your horse, in the here and now. If you drift off, thinking about yesterday or wondering about tomorrow, the connection disappears.

I had a client ask his horse to circle around him at a walk. After two circles, the horse stopped, though nothing had changed in the client's outward body language. He couldn't figure it out until asked what he was thinking about before the horse stopped. "About my family," he responded.

It always amazes people that horses can pick up on changes in mental focus. It all comes back to energy—thoughts are energy, and horses pick up on changes in the energy and where its directed.

If you are doing work in the arena and realize you have lost the connection, switch to doing something different and then go back to what you were doing before. When you are trail riding, keeping the connection will be more difficult.

I remember Ronnie Willis saying, "Whatever you have in the arena, you will have less than half [of the horse's attention] when you walk out that door because of the many distractions outside. Keep your horse's mind busy and this will impact its willingness to stay with you physically. The feet follow the mind."

In this situation, you might do some exercises similar to what you do in the arena. You might go sideways across a log, for example.

To me, connection is all about mutual respect. The biggest sign of respect we can give any living being with whom we are trying to communicate is to offer our full attention and listen with our hearts. How do you feel if you are talking to someone and sense that they aren't really listening? How do you respond? Horses and humans can look around while being together, but each needs to know where the other one is.

**"Never knock the curiosity out of a young horse."**

—Tom Dorrance

## Curiosity

"Curiosity is one of the three things you should never ruin in a horse," said Ronnie Willis. The other two are confidence and sensitivity.

Horses are naturally curious. Just watch them when you put a new object in the pasture. One by one they will go up to it, some quicker than others, depending on their level of confidence. Young horses are always curious.

It's up to you to keep your horse curious throughout its life. Do this by letting your horse explore things at its own pace. This might be something as simple as putting your saddle on the ground and allowing your horse to sniff and paw at it.

I've only done this with my Western saddle, making sure, of course, that I folded the stirrups under the saddle so the horse wouldn't get caught up in them. You can also let your horse sniff the saddle when it isn't on the ground. Often we put pads and saddles on a horse's back or a bridle on its head without ever giving it the chance to smell or come in contact with it first.

To keep the curiosity and learning going with my horse Hummer, I'd give him a horse treat anytime he put his nose onto something unfamiliar. When we rode through the forest, he would walk up to a pile of wood that hadn't been there last time, knowing I would reward him for his behavior. I always gave him the time he needed to approach a new object. If he just walked by it, that was fine, too.

Curiosity keeps horses in a learning frame of mind and open to new things.

The key is allowing them to discover and explore in a way that builds self-confidence.

**“All life deserves respect, dignity, and compassion.”**

—Anthony Douglas

## Dignity

A horseman once asked someone, "Would you treat the horse that way if your mother was watching?" I believe each living being has the right to be treated with dignity from the day it is born until the day it dies.

What does this mean in the life of a horse? For me, it begins with how horses are bred, when and how they are weaned from their mothers, how they grow up, when and how they are trained, stabled and ridden, and how they are cared for, especially as they get older and can no longer be ridden.

Anytime a horse becomes a means to end, dignity is at risk. If you see that a horse is not being treated correctly, please speak up for the sake of the horse.

Seek to understand the rider, ask questions, and share your observations. Just knowing that someone is watching may be enough to change their behavior.

**“Emotional intelligence allows us to consciously respond, instead of unconsciously react.”**

—Marina Parris

# Emotions

Humans and horses alike experience emotions that are triggered by outside circumstances or challenges in a relationship. In humans, though, our thoughts and the narratives we tell ourselves about what's happening can make things worse if we can't let the story go and return to a state of peaceful engagement with life.

Let's look at the emotions of fear, vulnerability, anger and frustration, for example, using the approach developed by Linda Kohanov, a pioneer and leader in equine-facilitated learning.

Based on her research into emotional intelligence, she found the work of author Karla McLaren particularly helpful in teaching people to recognize the message of an emotion and take action before that emotion intensifies and overwhelms us.

In her books *Becoming An Empath* and *The Language of Emotions,* McLaren encourages us to ask questions of emotions to determine what they are referring to in the present.

**Fear.** Someone approaching with an open umbrella can trigger fear in a horse. A horse can trigger fear in a human by going faster and faster. The message behind fear is that there is an external threat in the environment. Then you need to ask yourself, "What is the threat? And what must I do to move to a position of safety?" When you take action and move to safety, and then that fear will automatically subside. But if no action is taken, that fear will naturally intensify (from worry to anxiety to confusion to panic and all the way to dissociation), in both horses and humans, in order to get our attention.

A horse may spook or turn around as the person with the open umbrella approaches. A rider on an ever-faster horse may panic, jerk on the reins, or hold on with their legs.

The key is to recognize the emotion of fear before it intensifies and to take action accordingly. With the scary umbrella, you could stop the horse and get the attention of the person with the umbrella and ask them to close it. If this isn't possible, then simply turn around with your horse or make a really wide detour, far enough so the umbrella doesn't bother the horse. And in the case of a horse getting faster, you need to pick up on this right away and slow the horse down.

While it seems obvious that a frightened person would take action to feel safe, this isn't always the case. There are quite a few riders who won't admit to being scared, especially if they think they are the only ones in the group who feel that way (see Vulnerability). Imagine how a horse can feel with a scared rider, especially a less confident horse.

Since I started riding later in life, I was a cautious rider. In the beginning, I dismounted quite a bit because I felt I was a better leader on the ground than in the saddle if I encountered anything that scared me or my horse. My fear went away the moment I got off. Today both my horses and I are able to deal with most situations that we come across.

**Vulnerability.** This emotion often gets mixed up with fear. How often have you heard someone say they are scared of public speaking? What they really meant was is that public speaking would take them too far out of their comfort zone.

The message behind vulnerability is an internal threat to your self-image, belief system or comfortable habits. It's also about the fear of change, of experimenting, of trying something new.

The questions to be asked are "What belief, behavior, perception, or comfortable habit is being challenged?"; "How might my life change if I accept this new insight?"; and "Who can I go to for support in integrating this new insight?"

Going back to the example of a scared rider who doesn't take the necessary action (see Fear), it is often the feeling of vulnerability that stops this person from doing so. It's the concern about what other riders will think or say about them if they admit they are scared. As a result, these riders will make every effort to uphold the image to the outside world that they are a confident rider.

Vulnerability also often prevents riders from taking action when they are frustrated and things aren't working out (see Frustration). Here riders may be too embarrassed to ask for help because they worry about what others may think or say. They are, after all, experienced riders (self-image) and "should" be able to get their horses to do what they are asking.

Horses also experience vulnerability. I've seen an ex-racehorse experience this emotion in its new home. Here it had a pasture for the first time after being stabled in a single box for years. It took the horse about six weeks to get comfortable with the idea of leaving its stable (comfort zone) and walking directly out onto the pasture to graze.

**Anger.** Anger is a common emotion in both humans and horses. If a horse walks up and invades your space or pushes you around, you'll likely get angry. The message behind anger is that someone has overstepped a boundary with the conscious or unconscious intention of pushing you around, intimidating you or bending you to his/her will.

Karla McLaren recommends asking questions such as "What must be protected?" and "What boundary must be established or restored?"

Women often have a tough time setting boundaries with horses because they've been conditioned to care for everyone else first and therefore have difficulties standing up for their own needs. But worrying that they'll hurt the horse or that the horse won't like them is really just an excuse to avoid taking action.

When they can change their perspective to look at it from the horse's viewpoint, they find that it's natural for horses to claim their space when they are interacting with other horses.

Both people and horse may have to use considerable power to stand up to more dominant horses and/or people. In essence, the surge of energy felt as the anger rises within us, can be used to claim our space; horses do this instinctively.

When sensing anger, horses will first use nonviolent ways of communicating, like pinning their ears to warn the other horse to back off before resorting to kicking or biting to protect their space.

You initially see this behavior when you distribute piles of hay on the pasture even when there is enough hay and enough space in between the piles of hay. Once things are sorted out, the horses go back to grazing.

In stark contrast to humans, these horses won't need hours of counseling to work out their resentment and disappointment. Both offender and offended get the message behind the anger, change something in response, let the emotion go and resume their enjoyment of life.

If your emotions ever get too intense and you're so angry that you want to hit the horse, then stop, take a break and think of the situation from the horse's point of view.

**Frustration.** Frustration shows up as a block that keeps people and horses from achieving a goal. At first it may feel like anger to most people, but this emotion holds a completely different message. The message behind frustration is that the action you're taking is ineffective. To move forward you need to ask the following questions: "Where is the block?"; "What can I do differently?"; and "Whom can I go to for ideas or assistance?"

Riders may experience frustration when trying to get a horse to take the left lead, for example, and it just doesn't work. Most riders will just repeat the exercise and simply add more pressure on the horse while getting more emotional. Essentially, because they feel powerless and try to force the result. I've seen this repeatedly when observing riders in the arena and have experienced it myself in the past. Because I was frustrated and got emotional, I was not in the frame of mind to even think about what I could do differently and was too embarrassed to ask for help, especially as a riding instructor. So I tried to uphold the image that I should have all the answers and be able to solve any situation with a horse (see Vulnerability). Thankfully, I have come a long way, both with horses and in my personal life. Here are some examples of how horses experience frustration. Horses are hungry but can't eat, want to move but are in a stall, want to be with other horses but are stabled individually.

In contrast to humans, horses aren't in charge of their own destinies. When we ignore their needs, their "frustration" will show up as unwanted behavior—such as chewing on wood when they want to eat, weaving in the box because they need to move, or being jittery on a trail ride or in the arena because they don't get enough movement each day.

In the long run, ignoring their basic needs can also cause physical symptoms, such as ulcers. Ever wonder why ulcers are now common among recreational horses, not just sports horses? Too often we cause horses undue stress (frustration) by not respecting their natural needs when stabling and feeding them.

**Emotional intelligence.** Emotional intelligence gives us the opportunity to learn about ourselves by how we respond to what is going on around us. Having a constructive approach to dealing with emotions that trigger us will keep us from being overwhelmed by them and exploding or suppressing them as a result.

Horses deal with emotions in a natural manner. As Linda Kohanov states in her four-point approach to emotions, a horse will feel the emotion in its purest form, get the message behind the emotion, change something in response to the message, and then go back to grazing.

What does "go back to grazing" mean for us? What can we learn from the horses? We can learn to let go of our story, let go of the emotion and get back to what we were doing.

Emotional intelligence is an important skill that you need to gain—you owe it to your horse. A horse can forgive you much more easily if you use your emotions as information and interact with thoughtfulness and self-control. Try to be more like your horse.

Expressing emotions comes naturally to both horses and children. But at a certain age kids may begin to express emotions less and less because of parents who may say, "Johnny, don't be mean to your sister when she takes your toy." Or "Nancy, don't be scared, it's only a little dog." Because the need to be loved by parents is so strong, children may learn that it's not okay to express their true feelings. That's why many people go through life wearing a mask. When asked, they'll say they are fine, but inside they may be scared, vulnerable or angry. Linda Kohanov describes the situation quite well when she says, "Peace, love, and compassion can create social disharmony when worn like masks to cover unresolved anger, fear, sadness, and depression."

What happens in your body when you suppress an emotion? Basically, it's the same as when you try to hold a ball under water. Your blood pressure goes up, body tension increases, and breathing becomes shallow. It's difficult to focus on the task at hand because you're focusing on suppressing the emotion, also making it more difficult to connect with others. And don't forget the physical long-term consequences on your emotional and physical well-being.

Emotions are energy that's looking for expression. When suppressed, emotions form balls of energy in our body that can lead to illness, not to mention long-term unhappiness. It's important to note that studies also show that suppressing an emotion raises the blood pressure in those interacting with a person trying to hide his/her emotions.

**“Energy is the universal language of nature; nature is the universal source of information.”**

—Joey Lawsin

## Energy

Energy is our natural essence, and the natural essence of horses. When you go to get your horse from the pasture or its stall, it picks up on the energy coming from your heart. Your energy speaks to your horse before you've ever said a word.

Since energy is the universal language, it's something you can use to communicate with your horse. When I want to go from a walk to a trot, I first need to have a clear picture of what I want and then add energy to that picture to bring it to life—much like I'd turn up the volume on the radio. This increase in energy comes from my solar plexus, and I can use it for upward and downward transitions as well as to adjust the speed within a gait. If I want to trot more slowly, I can simply post at a slower pace. It's like going from a 6 down to a 4 on the volume control.

When teaching a horse to respond to your energy, give it enough time before you add physical cues. Let's say you want to go from a standstill to a walk. First have a clear picture of what you want and see it as already having happened. Then sit up in the saddle, look where you want to go, slowly take a deep breath and wait. If your horse doesn't understand you, gently squeeze with your legs. If it's not yet moving, tap its hindquarters every so lightly with the crop, keeping your legs on the horse, until it takes a step forward. Reward your horse right away by taking off all pressure—mentally and physically. And make sure you always do these steps in the same order.

Once the horse understands you, you'll need fewer and fewer steps for it to respond to your change in energy.

I have found that the more I use energetic forms of communication such as visualization, clarity, congruence, focus, or breathing, the fewer physical aids I need to rely on.

Most people continue to use physical aids and never tap into these other resources available to communicate with their horse. I see many people who squeeze with their legs for each step whether their horse is at a walk or trot. I just work with my own energy and teach the horse to match my energy level.

It's fun and easy to teach young horses to respond to your energy. We have both a two-year-old and a three-year-old on the farm, and I do races with them from the outside of the fence. I start running and vary the pace as I go along before slowing back down to a walk and then stopping. They beautifully match my energy. Once we've stopped, I pet or give them each a horse treat. It's a playful and fun way to teach horses to respond to your level of energy.

Sometimes my horse Riverdance has more energy than I'm asking for—when I lunge her, for instance. I ask for a trot, but she takes off at a canter. At times I ignore this, knowing she'll come back down to a trot and we can continue from there. At other times I redirect that energy and ask her to go over poles on the ground. That way she has to pay more attention and can't just run around.

**"You can't teach feel, you have to experience it."**

—Bill Dorrance

## Feel

Feel is as elusive as connection. Two riders may ask the same horse to go sideways, and the first rider gets the job done but with obvious resistance from the horse. The second rider also gets the job done, but the process is a lot smoother because the horse isn't resisting. What's the difference? The difference is in how much feel each rider has offered the horse. Sometimes it's just a matter of waiting a bit longer to really feel and connect with the horse before you move forward together.

You must learn to feel where your horse is at mentally, emotionally and physically before asking it to do something. Once you have its attention, you can ask your question and move forward together. If you don't know where it's at, your horse will just react because you caught it off guard.

Since feel can be a challenge to teach, I often let people work with my own horses. This helps them get a feel for what they are working toward and recognize when their horses respond to a feel.

Feel is everywhere. It shows up in how you approach a horse, stroke it, put a halter on, lead it, groom it and so on.

The easiest way to see if someone has feel is to watch them when they approach and pet a horse in an open area. A horse will normally stand still if someone approaches with feel and allow that person to pet it. I guess it's because horses are so big that people often think they have to "pat" instead of "pet" a horse, not knowing how highly sensitive these animals are to touch.

I teach kids and adults that the best way to pet a horse is to imagine your heart in the palm of your hand and then gently pet the horse. This way of stroking a horse helps build connection, because it feels good to the horse. It can remind the horse of the way it was licked by its mother.

**"Where focus goes, energy flows."**

—Tony Robbins

## Focus

If you want to observe just how powerful focus is and how it affects precision of movement, watch how straight a horse walks when you head back toward the stable. Then notice how that same "straight" horse becomes crooked as you ride away from the stable because its focus is still on the stable.

A horse will more naturally focus when it has a sense of purpose. When I was in Montana and we regularly moved herds of horses and sometimes even Black Angus cows, we had a job to do—keep the herd together—and thus had a clear focus. Every move was filled with a sense of purpose, whether this meant going faster, backing off or moving a bit more to the right. So how can you build purpose into what you do with your horse, even if you don't live on a working ranch?

As an alternative to standing still when you are lunging a horse, try walking around while it is circling you and have it go over or around various obstacles (tarp, poles, carpet, barrels, umbrella, and so on). This is a way to keep the horse focused, because now it has to watch where it puts its feet.

Another fun thing to do in the arena is to ride behind another rider and do exactly what they do, and then switch roles. You can do this at either a walk or a trot.

Focus is important regarding what *you* want, too. Sounds easy, but often we focus on what we *don't* want instead of what we want.

I once had a woman in a riding lesson who wanted to ride along the arena railing at a walk. Her horse had other ideas, however, and wanted to turn toward the middle of the arena. She became frustrated and kept trying to use her leg and reins to get her horse back to the rail, to no avail. I asked her to stop for a moment and tell me what she was focusing on. She responded, "I was doing everything I could to keep the horse from going toward the center of the arena."

What did you want, I asked. "I want my horse to ride straight along the rail." Her focus was on what she *didn't* want instead of what she wanted, and the horse was simply responding to what she was focusing on. So I asked her to imagine riding in front of Queen Elizabeth—an avid horsewoman—and to stay focused on her goal, even if the horse tried to change her focus. Those two changes were all it took. The horse stayed on the rail perfectly, as if to say, "Oh, is this what you wanted?"

Focus is also important when you're trail riding. Some horses enjoy snacking along the way; usually this only happens if it's an existing habit. I experienced this a lot when I worked as a wrangler and led trail rides with riders who were completely inexperienced with horses. We had totally safe horses, but every horse knew exactly what kind of rider sat on top. Once a horse started snacking, the rider usually looked down to where it was eating and struggled to get the horse back on the trail. But if the rider changed the focus toward where he or she wanted to go and added some forward energy, the horse usually went along with the idea.

**"For to be free is to live in a way that enhances the freedom of others."**

—Nelson Mandela

# Freedom

We need to give a horse the freedom to be a horse. We need to give it freedom to move and to express itself, and the freedom to be itself while discovering and exploring life together with us.

**Freedom to move.** Movement is essential to horses; it makes up two-thirds of their day in the wild. Do what you can to give your horse freedom of movement 24/7. The result will be a happier horse.

**Freedom to express.** Spending time with wild horses and observing family members interact with one another will soon make you realize that horses aren't as different from humans as we often make them out to be. They may look, think and behave differently, but in the end, they are sentient beings as much as we are. They, too, thrive when they are together.

**Freedom to be.** Make sure that your horse's personality can shine through in whatever you do together. This means not trying to change a horse to fit some kind of preconceived idea you have in your head about how a horse should be or behave.

**"People rarely succeed unless they are having fun in what they are doing."**

—Dale Carnegie

## Fun

One day while riding in an open field I wanted to try something fun. I was riding Hummer and ponying Riverdance, leading her alongside. I'd done this a few times before and had noticed that it went even easier when she was in heat, because then she stuck to Hummer like glue. This seemed like a good day to incorporate Mother Nature into my fun idea, so instead of ponying Riverdance, I just let her free—and she loved it! She trotted and then cantered alongside us before bucking around from pure joy! I'm glad that Hummer stayed calm while Riverdance happily ran around—I don't think I'd have tried this idea the other way around!

One day I thought it would be cool if I could teach Hummer to rear. A friend helped me get started, and he figured it out pretty quickly. On the days when we did groundwork and the weather was cool, he had more energy and it took little for him to go up on his hindquarters—quite an impressive sight.

Jogging with your horse can be a lot of fun, too. It offers a change of pace for both horse and rider. Most of the time Hummer and Riverdance are happy to stay at the pace of their two-legged friend. However, when they are full of energy, I tend to do sprints and then take a break again, while they happily graze.

What are some fun things you can do with your horse?

**"Oh! If people knew what a comfort to a horse a light hand is."**

—Anna Sewell

## Give and Take

Some people have the funny notion that just because they pay for the stabling costs and all the other expenses related to having a horse, their horse owes them something in return and they have a right to take what they want from it. This is purely a human notion; horses don't operate like that.

How do you like "friends" who only call when they need something from you? Not much fun to have as friends. Many people treat their horses like that. They only come to see the horse when they want something from it, like going on a trail ride, working in the arena or taking part in a competition.

On the other hand, there are friends who call just to say "hi" and to see how you are doing, or they may come over for a cup of coffee. How often do you visit your horse just to say "hi"? It's good for a relationship to have a healthy mix of give and take.

Give and take also applies to the qualities we want our horse to develop. Mahatma Ghandi once said, "We must be the change we seek in the world," and that wisdom applies to the horse world as well.

If your dance partner is smooth, then you will most likely respond in the same manner. If your dance partner is rough and uncoordinated, then you may end up like that as well.

In other words, you must offer the horse what you want it to become. If you desire a balanced horse, physically, emotionally, and mentally, then it makes sense that you are first balanced in these areas. If you want a soft horse, you need to offer softness in everything you do with a horse—with your hands, your legs and your seat. Because every part of the horse is connected to its mind, a soft horse willingly responds to the slightest signals of the rider.

As Ronnie Willis always said, "Asking a horse to do things should be as easy as pushing a plastic duck in the water."

If you offer lightness, then the horse will respond with lightness. If you offer heaviness, then the horse will resist and become heavy, simply reflecting your own behavior back to you. Lightness begins in your mind, it's a choice you make.

**"If the plan doesn't work, change the plan, but not necessarily the goal."**

—Author Unknown

## Goals

Goals are easy to have but not always so easy to implement when they involve others. We don't want to force our goals onto a horse, no more than we want to have a boss telling us what we need to be doing all the time. The challenge lies in getting your horse to share your goals and go on the journey with you.

Regardless of what goal you choose, *how* you achieve the goal is even more important to your horse than the goal itself. Are you able to park your ego at the door and work with the horse in such a way that it feels good about itself and what's going on, on the way to the goal? The mental and emotional states of your horse are important, as they are reflected in the way a horse responds to you and how it moves its body.

Before you get started on a bigger goal, think about how much it really means to you. Is it something you really want deep inside, or are you simply doing it because everyone else is?

Anything you do from the heart will draw people and horses to you, as your enthusiasm will be contagious. Both people and horses feel more comfortable when they are around positive people.

Once you've figured out what you want, you need to get your horse on board. Do you remember liking or disliking a subject in school just because of your teacher? Usually it came down to how they presented the material to you and supported you in the learning process. It's no different with horses. It's all about *how* you present things to your horse and *when* you reward your horse, so that it stays motivated and open to learning new things as both of you move toward your goal.

Pay attention to and care about your horse's attitude along the way—is it bored, interested or maybe really into what you're doing together? Its attitude could be valuable feedback for you.

In the end, your horse cares more about how you reach the goal *together* than what it achieves with you. Strive for progress and not perfection each day.

"If we are not a little bit uncomfortable every day, we are not growing. All the good stuff is outside our comfort zone."

—Jack Canfield

## Growth

At the beginning of this book, I talked about the importance of moving up to where a horse is and not bringing the horse down to where we as riders are—physically, emotionally and mentally. This means moving out of our own comfort zone to where personal growth can take place.

As you grow, your horse can grow with you. Many people never tap into their own potential and that of the horse because they won't inconvenience themselves to step outside of their comfort zone.

On a scale of 1 to 10, when you or your horse feels comfortable you are in your comfort zone, between 1 and 3.

Once you or your horse get out of that comfort zone in order to learn new things, you're between 4 and 6.

If you and/or your horse are forced to do things you're not ready for, then you're in the panic zone—between 7 and 10. Learning can no longer take place, because now fear dominates and triggers the survival instinct—not to mention the impact this has on trust.

When I first started taking riding lessons, I was scared most of the time, especially while jumping or cantering in a group. I was just happy to make it through each lesson and never really liked the teacher. I stopped taking lessons after a few weeks because this wasn't the way I wanted to learn and be around horses.

When I first got Riverdance, I wondered how I was ever going to ride her at a canter. Although she was very soft and sensitive, as a Thoroughbred mix, she loved to move somewhat faster than my comfort zone allowed for at that point. So I had the choice of getting Riverdance to be more like my Quarter Horse, Hummer, relaxed in all gaits, or going up to her level, relaxed but at a somewhat faster pace. Because I wanted her to get the exercise she so enjoyed and not get bored while I was learning, I had a more experienced young gal ride her. That way she had a rider who could work with her where she was at while I was working on expanding my own comfort zone. It was a win-win situation all around.

If you want to continue to learn and grow, you will try new things or perhaps do the same thing in a different place—like trotting sideways in an open field instead of in the arena. Remember, your horse can only grow to the extent that you are willing to step outside of your own comfort zone.

Think about the time with your horse and ask yourself, "How much time do I spend in the comfort zone and how much time do I spend in the learning zone?" Answer both for yourself and for your horse.

**"There is no sense of time when learning the skill of extended sensory awareness with horses. You are in Horse Consciousness."**

—Kathy Pike

## Hanging Out

Have you ever observed a herd of horses for an extended amount of time? How much time do they spend interacting with other herd members, grazing or simply just standing next to each other?

If you find it hard to do nothing around your horse, here's a wonderful exercise for you. Spend 20 minutes with your horse loose in a pen or arena. Just sit on a chair and do nothing—don't even touch the horse when it comes up to you. What do you discover about yourself, about your horse?

This exercise is a pleasant change for the horse, too. Going into an arena or pen usually means work, but now it's also a place to roll around, explore and be with the human in a different way. Don't do it just once. This can be a practical way to spend time with your horse if you've had a long day at work and aren't in the frame of mind to work with it.

"Hanging out" is valuable for strengthening your relationship with the horse. I don't ride or do groundwork every time I go to my horses. Sometimes I just watch them, groom them in the pasture or take them out to go grazing.

Hanging out together is very important when you're beginning a new relationship. I often see people who've just bought a horse be out and about working with it the very next day. When I first got Riverdance, I spent the first couple of weeks just getting her out, grooming her and going for walks to explore the new surroundings, until she felt more and more comfortable leaving the stables and going for walks alone with me.

Horses need time to adjust to a new home, new herd members and new caretakers, and it's essential to give them this time. Just hanging out with a horse is especially important if it has had a difficult past, since it needs to learn to trust humans again.

**“He who lives in harmony with himself lives in harmony with the universe.”**

—Marcus Aurelius

## Harmony

Have you ever watched two horses running and playing with each other? Did you notice how their movements mirror one another? They are both on the same lead, they both turn in the same direction, they both stop and take a break. They act as one.

I have experienced many such moments with my horses. Sometimes I feel it on the ground when I run over or around obstacles in the arena with my horse beside me or when I go jogging with my horses. When I canter Riverdance outdoors, I feel like I'm flying on the wings of my horse. Everything is light, effortless, flowing, and I feel totally connected to my horse.

The feeling is hard to describe. Sometime it lasts for only a quick moment and other times longer, but you will certainly know when you are in this sweet spot. You can't look for it, you can't make it happen, but you carry this possibility in your heart, knowing it will come about when the moment is right.

If this is what you want with your horse, you must believe that it's possible. If you seek harmony, you will achieve it. One exercise I learned a long time ago was to mirror my horse on the ground. I stopped when it stopped, moved when it moved, and looked where it looked. This is a fun exercise to do at any time, and I find that it helps me see the world from the horse's perspective.

Another way I discovered to get a feel of harmony was to walk next to Hummer or Riverdance and put my hand on different body parts (back, hips, ribs) to see how they moved. Observing a horse walk and feeling it walk are two different things. Try it for yourself to feel the difference. Do this with your eyes closed and you'll get an even better feel for the horse. Try it with two or three horses to feel how differently each one moves. During riding lessons, I have people close their eyes while I lead them around at a walk. It helps them get a feel for how a horse turns, goes backward, stops and starts moving again, and they begin to learn to follow the movement of their horse.

Being in harmony is like being in love. It's an indescribable feeling between two beings that cannot be captured in words. You feel when it's there and you feel when it's not there. Where do you experience harmony with *your* horse?

**“Our goal is to get as close to being its mother as possible.”**

—Ronnie Willis

## Leadership

I like to think of leadership as the horse choosing to follow my lead because of the respect and trust it has in me. It is a choice the horse makes in every moment because of the relationship we have.

We often take it for granted that a horse will follow the lead of a species that pales in comparison to its own physical power and mental strength. But when we are prepared to go on the inward journey to earn the respect and trust of a horse, it rewards us in so many ways.

What determines whether a horse follows you isn't so much about what you do with your horse, but how you treat it. A horse must know that you, as a leader, will never do anything to cause it harm in any way (see the section on Trust).

When you treat your horse with respect, day in and day out, you demonstrate to the horse that it is safe and can relax in your presence.

Given this kind of relationship with my own horses, they have freedom to provide input and make decisions. I always ensure that neither my safety nor theirs gets compromised. For example, I'll let the horse change gait or direction, but it's a conscious choice on my part, and that's what makes the difference. If I feel a horse wants to canter, I can stay one step ahead and cue it to canter. Or if I sense that a horse is just feeling good today, I'll let it change gaits. If you know your horse well, you'll be able to sense whether it is trying to take over or just expressing a need!

When it comes to leadership, this is one of my favorite sayings from Ronnie Willis: "Sit on your horse like you are going somewhere, not like you are lost on top of him."

I don't remember where I heard about GPS—goal, path, and speed—but I find it a great tool to help better understand leadership and recognize who has the lead, you or your horse. Ideally, you as a leader define what you want (goal), you decide how to get there (path) and then you determine how fast you want to travel (speed). There will always be times when the horse takes over one of these three elements. If it takes over two out of three of them, though, the alarm bells should go off—and if it has taken over all three, it's fully in charge and has momentarily taken over the lead.

I also remember Ronnie saying, "Horses learn from leadership, but also from the absence of leadership. Horses will not try to take over if someone is already in charge."

As with anything in life, there are always exceptions, or horses that will try to take over even if you are already in charge. While it's a fact that horses naturally dominate, it's not an ego power play as it often is in the human world. They just need to know who's running the show—you or them?

I have found the five leadership roles defined by Linda Kohanov to be extremely valuable. I refer to them not only in my coaching work, as it relates to people taking responsibility for their lives, but also when I give riding lessons.

I have taken the five roles from Linda's book *The Five Roles of a Master Herder* to demonstrate their use in the horse world, using the mature and immature forms of power that Linda describes in her book.

The successful use of these five roles depends on your ability to embrace the use of mature power to influence your horse.

The mature use of each role in the human world can be characterized as coming from the heart, and an immature use of the role as coming from an unhealthy ego.

Your ability to move fluidly among the first four roles, not overemphasizing one or avoiding another, will influence your success as a rider. The result will be a horse that follows and is soft and fluid in movement, since there is little inner resistance. Just look at wild horses and how relaxed they are when following the lead mare.

Horses rarely use the predator role, though they can injure or kill another horse or attacking predator if need be. It is also a role that, hopefully, you use rarely.

| Role | Mature | Immature |
|---|---|---|
| **Dominant**<br><br>Direct and protect:<br>dominance without malice | Dominance is used to set boundaries and protect one's own needs. It's also used to break through resistance assertively, not aggressively. | Dominance is used as a power play to show who is in charge. |
| **Leader**<br><br>Discover and inspire:<br>leadership through relationship | Leadership is established through trust and respect. Your horse is your partner, and the quality of your relationship is more important than any goal. | Leadership is established almost exclusively through dominance. The horse becomes a means to an end to achieve your goals. |
| **Nurturer**<br><br>Support and connect:<br>the power of companionship | Caring is used to strengthen the relationship with your horse. You are willing to see situations from your horse's perspective. | Caring is aimed at your own well-being at the expense of your horse. |
| **Sentinel**<br><br>Observe and alert:<br>the sentinel's perspective | You have awareness of both self and the horse, so you can know how to respond in every moment. | You watch the horse to look for mistakes, in order to correct it —a form of control. |
| **Predator**<br><br>Cull and recalibrate:<br>the predator's sacred task | If you realize this isn't the right horse for you or you can no longer have a horse for whatever reason, it's in both of your interests to find a new home for it. You may also have to let go of a horse when it needs to be put down. All this is done with the utmost respect and dignity. | If the horse doesn't perform to expectations, you sell it and get another one—only to experience the same problems again. |

Chart used with permission from *The Five Roles of a Master Herder,* by Linda Kohanov © 2016

**“What we can learn from horses is infinitely more valuable than what we can teach them.”**

—Author Unknown

## Learning

When your horse is learning new things, it's helpful to keep in mind the three zones defined under the section on Growth. On a scale of 1 to 10, the comfort zone is 1 to 3, the learning zone 4 to 6 and the panic zone 7 to 10.

If your horse has a glazed-over look when you do things with it, it's safe to say that you're spending too much time in its comfort zone and your horse is no longer learning anything new. I've observed people riding on the same trail or repeating the same exercises day in and day out, adding nothing new or exciting. It's no wonder these horses are bored and have that glazed-over look.

Horses are used to taking part in life mentally, emotionally and physically. If they get bored, you risk unwanted behaviors—such as aggressiveness or dominance, or shutting down inside, depending on what kind of horse you have.

Growth and learning for both people and horses takes place outside the comfort zone. Just grooming the horse in a different setting is a starting point, so that your horse learns to be comfortable being groomed regardless of where you do it. Or try teaching your horse to stand still while grooming so you don't have to tie it up. Pay attention to how much keeping the horse in its comfort zone relates to your *unwillingness* to get out of your own comfort zone or change an existing habit.

Once you step into the learning zone, know that there's no such thing as failure, only new experiences. Just think about how you can do it differently next time and change your behavior accordingly.

Remember, both you and your horse are always doing the best you can with what you have. If you aren't getting the results you expected, don't blame the horse; find another way to communicate what you want. Asking for help is always a great way to go. Sometimes a fresh pair of eyes will spot the issue right away.

**"Until one has loved an animal, a part of one's soul remains unawakened."**

—Anatole France

## Love

Love has the power to overcome many obstacles in life. Riverdance wasn't in great shape when I got her, and a lot of health issues came up in the first two years. That made riding for long periods impossible. That didn't matter to me—I had plenty of other ways to spend our time together. I always knew that once she was completely healthy, she would simply be outstanding, and to this day she continues to amaze me in so many ways. Riverdance has danced her way into the hearts of many people who have learned from and with her.

Thanks to horses, I also learned what unconditional love meant. I felt what it was like to love unconditionally and to be loved unconditionally. My horses did not care what I looked like on the outside—my hairstyle, whether my socks matched or if I had make-up on. They cared about the person I was on the inside, deep in my heart. They cared about the quality of our time together and the deep connection that we shared. I think that's why so many people are drawn to animals. Because they carry no judgment, we can simply be who we are and still be loved.

**"It is not about flying lead changes, but about a horse coming to you because he wants to be with you."**

—Dave Stuart

## Partnership

The goal of having your horse be your partner begins in your head. It starts with seeing the horse as an equal. This means a willingness to work with your horse at eye level and to accept and respect its opinions. It means that your horse can say "no" or "not like that" when you ask it to do something. A horse must always be able to express itself and know that you will listen and change something as necessary.

Let me give you two examples. My horses usually come to me, curious about what we'll do together. On rare occasions, though, Hummer didn't come. At first I'd go to him and put a halter on, but he didn't budge. The message was a clear "no," for whatever reason. So I took the halter off and either hung out for a while or went back home.

When I went riding with Riverdance, I usually knew what trail I wanted to take, but at times Riverdance would insist on going another way. As the relationship was solid, I didn't worry about her "taking over" and we'd go down the trail she wanted. I wouldn't suggest letting a horse decide too much until you have a strong relationship going, but you can begin by giving your horse a say in smaller matters—which obstacle it wants to approach first when doing groundwork, say, the plastic tarp or walking between the barrels.

I am always open to, though not always amused by, what my horses have to say. When I did groundwork with Hummer in the arena and he did not have a halter on and he'd had enough, he would just walk over to the gate and stand there. I guess it wasn't interesting enough for him to continue. What I love about Hummer is how clear he is. There's no room for misunderstanding!

Horses ask a lot of questions—can we go here, can I do that, are you sure about this? Every time a horse asks you a question, it's an opportunity to have a conversation. Dialogue is essential to any true partnership.

**"Breathing deeply while in the presence of a horse can completely transform how one experiences the moment."**

—Kathy Pike

## Presence

Being in the presence of horses can do wonders for us humans. It's as if time stops and we step into another world. Sometimes we are drawn to a particular horse and just silently stand in its presence. I believe that being in the presence of horses enables us to connect with our true essence, our divine nature, and that of the horse.

I had a coaching client who was so deeply moved by such an experience with a horse that she began to cry. She was reconnecting with her divine essence that had been dormant for years and was now yearning to be expressed again.

Another coaching client, as she sat with Hummer in a large outdoor pen, remembered an unrealized dream that she'd been carrying in her heart.

And I got the title for this book one evening as I was standing next to Hummer out in the pasture. I was telling him about the book, where I was at with it and when it would be published. He just stood there licking and chewing when suddenly the book title popped into my head.

When have you felt the true presence of your horse? This is something that can only be felt when you go beyond the physical senses.

Humans have a divine nature. We come in contact with it most easily when we are around human or animal babies or out in nature. Those are moments when time doesn't exist and our hearts are wide open. That is our true nature. Encountering and working with horses from this perspective is a game changer, and you access this state by entering into the present moment.

Being drawn to a particular horse often goes way beyond its physical appearance. There is just "something" that you sense, but cannot name. Then you are tapping into the essence of the horse, or the spirit of the horse.

**"Realize deeply that the present moment is all you ever have."**

—Eckhart Tolle

## Present Moment

Your mind can only be in one of three places at any moment—the past, the present or the future. Considering that horses only know and live in the present, that's where you need to be as well. If your attention drifts off into the past or the future, then who is there for the horse? No one.

Some confident horses are okay if you drift off. But horses like Riverdance, who are less confident in certain situations and looking for guidance, can become troubled in that situation. They need you, or else they'll get lost and can take over in order to look after their own interests—a perfectly natural response. Even a confident horse like Hummer can take over and find better things to do with his time if no one is there to run the show.

Being present has to do with respect, too. Why should a horse attempt to stay focused and connected to you when your attention isn't on the horse?

It's the same with people. It can be quite annoying when you're talking to someone, only to realize that they aren't really listening.

That's one reason that I often go riding alone. I can talk to people all day long, but the time with my horses is precious and I don't want to miss out on the conversation with them.

When people ride together and talk the whole time, it seems like the horse is more a mode of transportation than a genuine friend with whom you have a conversation with.

When you only focus on the future and compare your horse today to where you want it to be, you can easily run into a problem. More often than not, your horse isn't the same as it was yesterday—mentally, emotionally, and physically. Yesterday your horse easily went sideways across the pole, while today the same task is more difficult. What changed? Are you in the same frame of mind—do you feel the same emotionally and physically as yesterday, and does your horse? And how do you know?

Instead of analyzing the situation, simply deal with where you and your horse are at this given moment and go from there, regardless of how good or bad things were the day before. Stay positive and know that you will achieve your goals together.

When you focus on the past it can also be a problem for your horse. You worry that your horse will spook again in a certain corner of the arena. You tense up as you approach that corner, and the horse senses your tension and mirrors you. How about consciously choosing another response, such as relaxation through deep breathing, or visualizing what you want instead of what you don't want.

I had a client who for years had trouble getting past a certain object, because each time she had mental images of her horse refusing to go by. When she changed the mental images to what she wanted right now and focused on deep breathing to keep her in the present moment, she was able to pass without a problem.

Deep breathing will not only bring you into the present moment and relax you, but also communicate to your horse that everything is okay.

Breathing will always be the key to entering the present moment where your horse lives—a place where your mind stops thinking and your body begins sensing.

**"Too many people want to solve a problem without looking at what is causing it!"**

—Ray Hunt

## Problems

I believe that most problems with horses are self-made because we don't truly understand their nature, are unwilling to see things from their perspective or are unwilling to change our own behaviors and ways of thinking to accommodate the horse.

A horse that is misbehaving in the eyes of a human is trying to tell us something, and we need to try to figure it out what that is. As Ray Hunt has said, "A horse does one of two things. He does what he thinks he is supposed to do. Or he does what he thinks he needs to do to survive."

It is easy to blame a horse and assume it simply doesn't want to do something, but we are only deceiving ourselves by blaming the horse.

If a horse doesn't do something, it has a good reason—or many reasons. For example, the rider didn't communicate clearly, didn't properly prepare the horse for the task, got in the way, didn't have the necessary respect or trust. Or the horse has a physical problem that the rider may be unaware of—teeth problems, poor-fitting tack, or a health issue that needs to be addressed by a professional.

What we tend to label as a difficult horse is just one that doesn't do what we want. Sometimes those difficult horses can be our best teachers because they "force" us to grow, to rethink things and find a new way.

A horse has no choice but to get "louder" with its behavior in order to get the rider's attention that something isn't right. Maybe it's time to listen more closely to what your horse is trying to tell you.

**"When you do something with purpose, you put your heart and soul into it."**

—Unknown Author

## Purpose

What I loved most about my time on the ranch in Montana was that everything we did with the horses had a purpose. We rode the fences each morning to make sure nothing had happened overnight; rode through the herds each day to check each horse for injuries or changes; rode faster or slower as we moved a herd of horses or cattle, to keep them together.

We were definitely a team. What we did had a purpose and meaning for both of us, not to mention the fun we had doing it!

While most of us don't live in this kind of setting, we should still try to put purpose and meaning in what we do with our horses. This can be as simple as adding obstacles to whatever task you're doing in the arena, maybe going sideways over a pole or barrel or backward through poles placed in an L-shape pattern. Or you could ride the same obstacles at both a walk and a trot while holding a cup of water in one hand. Go over and through natural obstacles on trail rides to make it more interesting for both you and your horse. Get creative, and have fun!

**"I stop thinking. Swim in silence and the truth comes to me."**

—Albert Einstein

## Questions

Often when I asked a certain instructor a question, his first response was, "It depends." This was rather frustrating when I just wanted a solution so that I could continue doing what I was doing.

But since then, I often find myself responding to clients' questions with "It depends" or "Why don't you show me what you are doing with your horse?"

Each horse-and-rider situation is unique. As a result, there are no "cut and paste" answers. What works for one won't necessarily work for another. If a horse is hesitating to go backward, it could be because of how the rider is asking or because the horse is aware of an object behind it. By watching someone with their horse, I can get the horse's perspective on the situation by observing its behavior.

I have also learned to respond with a question when a rider asks me something like "Why isn't my horse stopping where I want?"

This is because I know that riders often have the answers inside, even though it may not be obvious to them at first. But if I can get them to pay more attention to what the horse is saying and take the time to look for answers in themselves, they will get better and better at this.

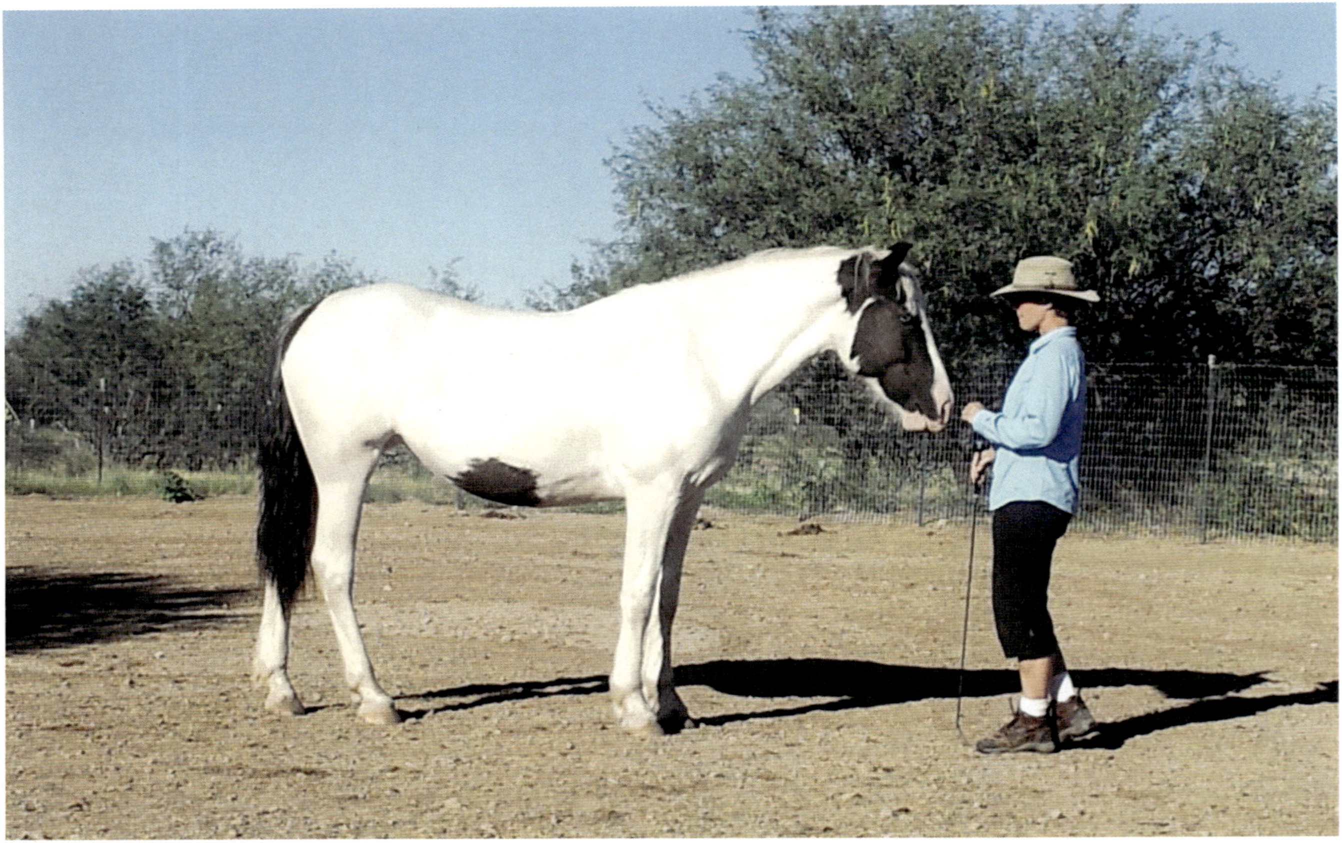

**“The horse needs to respect you, but sometimes people confuse respect and fear. And they’re not the same at all.”**

—Buck Brannaman

## Respect

Respectful or disrespectful? People tend to judge and label everything, but a horse doesn't understand the concept of respect. As Ray Hunt says, "A horse only does what it has been taught to do or what it feels it needs to do to survive."

Riders can be quick to label their horse as disrespectful, but the unwanted behavior is what they have unknowingly taught the horse. Blaming the horse is easy, but it often doesn't address the real problem—the human.

As a rider, you need to be able to differentiate between a scared horse and one that's exhibiting unwanted behavior. A scared or nervous horse will have its eyes wide open, lips tight, head carried high and muscles tensed. It usually has to move its feet and may even feel the need to defend itself if it cannot flee. The motivation of every living being is to be free of fear.

A horse displaying unwanted behavior will invade your space, be pushy, perhaps nip at you, or refuse to do something. This might be funny or cute at first, but it can easily turn into a bigger problem if you don't address it right away.

I experienced this with Riverdance, when a gentle nudge for one more horse treat turned into a powerful push with her head. Her unwanted behavior was like a weed in the vegetable garden that spread because it took me too long to do something about it.

How you read your horse will determine how you respond.

A scared horse requires safety and comfort, while a horse showing unwanted behavior needs more clarity on your part and some thought as to why your horse is behaving the way it is.

To earn the respect of your horse, you must be fair, consistent, and clear. You need to be clear in your own mind about what behavior you want and don't want from the horse.

If it doesn't matter to you, it won't matter to the horse.

As Ronnie Willis always said, "A horse should give you the same respect it gave its mother."

This applies when it comes to leading a horse, too. You don't lead a horse; it follows you out of respect.

A simple way to lose respect is to ask a horse to do something that it's not capable of either mentally, emotionally, or physically. This is setting your horse up for failure.

Always be conscious of your actions and know whether you are building or losing respect with your horse. It's not about being perfect, it's about becoming aware.

Know that when you gain respect in one area with your horse, that this will contribute to the overall respect a horse has for you.

**"The horse is a gift to us, to humanity. And for that, there comes responsibility. If the horse is gonna work for you and work with you, then the best thing I can do for the horse is to make as good a life as possible."**

—Buck Brannaman

## Responsibility

Owning a horse is a big commitment and responsibility over the lifetime of the horse. Basically, you have the responsibility for the well-being of your horse 24/7, much the same as when you have kids.

If something isn't right where the horse is being stabled, you must speak up and be the voice of your horse. It can only speak to us through its behavior. If the stable owners aren't willing to listen, it's time to look for a new place.

I used to teach at a stable where the well-being of the horse was top priority. Then the ownership changed hands. They enlarged the operations and hired young apprentices. When one apprentice was told to slow down with a particular horse he was leading because it was older and had trouble walking, the answer was, "I don't have time to walk slower."

I knew of a horse with back problems because its saddle didn't fit and the owner was overweight. Instead of making the obvious change, she hired someone to massage her horse. This horse continued to suffer in silence.

Other horses might not tolerate such pain and won't stand still when being saddled or mounted. Instead of forcing a horse to stand still, you need to notice any change in behavior and search for answers.

A horse can only make you aware of a problem; it's up to you to find a solution that fits the horse. We always need to reflect on whether we are part of the problem or part of the solution.

If you see a horse being treated unfairly, try to enter a dialogue with the person involved in order to understand what's happening. This can be very helpful before addressing what you've observed.

Be the voice of the horse wherever you go. I know it can be uncomfortable, but knowing I can make a difference to that one horse has given me the courage to speak up.

**"Always look for a place to reward the horse."**

—Author Unknown

## Reward

For a reward to be meaningful, it has to be given instantaneously, so that the horse can link the reward to its own behavior. Therefore your attention needs to be on the horse, so as not to miss any effort on its part to do what you are asking.

You can reward a horse's behavior in so many different ways. The easiest is to use your voice, which can be helpful when you're at a distance or you have your hands full. Another way is to stop and take a break when your horse does what you asked, giving it some time to process what it has just learned. You can gently stroke your horse, give it a treat, move onto another exercise, or put the horse back into its herd.

Because mares lick their foals, stroking your horse while imagining your heart in your hand will feel more like a reward to the horse than patting it as you would a dog.

Rewarding correctly involves two things: having a goal, and having perfect timing. For your timing to be perfect, you must first know what goal you are trying to achieve, so you can reward your horse for each try, for each step toward that goal. How else is it going to know that it is on the right track?

When I'm teaching a horse something new, I need to recognize when it has understood me and tried to do what I've asked.

If I'm teaching a young horse to give me its foot, I will reward any attempt to lift that foot. At first this may simply mean that the horse shifts its weight in order to prepare to give me its foot. If I don't recognize and immediately reward the slightest effort of the horse to understand me, it will look for a different solution and we will have nothing to build on.

You must always be aware in what moment you reward a horse because that is the behavior you are encouraging.

Let's say my goal is for the horse to easily give me its foot for cleaning. If I pick up the foot to clean it, my horse pulls it away and I let go, I'm rewarding behavior I don't want.

Instead, unless it's a safety issue, I simply go with the movement of the foot and then when I feel the horse relax, even for just a moment, I release the foot. If later on the horse pulls its foot away again, for whatever reason, I simply pick it up again and release it the second it is light in my hand.

I find treats helpful in the beginning for more challenging things, such as loading a horse into a trailer or walking over plastic tarps. Treats can help horses overcome those first "scary" steps. At the end of a day, though, a horse should be able to walk into a trailer or do anything else, for that matter, without a treat.

Treats were helpful when Hummer was afraid of new objects after he'd first moved to Switzerland. I conditioned him to approach and put his nose on unfamiliar objects—such as a tarp or a pile of wood or an umbrella—by rewarding him with a treat. In the end, he started looking for unfamiliar objects, knowing he'd get a treat.

Being clear in your head about what you want makes it easier to reward desired behavior.

**"In riding a horse, we borrow freedom."**

—Helen Thompson

## Saddle

Your horse's saddle is like your shoes. If your shoes don't fit perfectly, you won't want to wear them because they are uncomfortable. And if you do, you will move differently. The same applies to your horse's saddle. Your horse is the only one who can tell you—by how it moves—whether or not the saddle and padding work for it.

Saddles often are too small for a horse, because we fit them when the horse is standing still. But how much does a horse's shoulder blade move when the horse moves?

Both Western and English saddles will influence the horse's movement if they don't fit properly. A Western saddle might push a shoulder forward, while an English saddle can cause more pronounced withers because the muscles underneath will atrophy if the saddle is not correctly fitted.

While I enjoy my Western saddle, I don't feel the horse's movement as well as when I use my English saddle, nor do I feel that Hummer can move as freely. Riding with an English saddle was a challenge at first. I felt as if I'd never ridden before! That was when I really understood what it meant to have an independent seat.

You should regularly check your saddle. For example, the saddle cushions may not provide the same level of comfort as when they were new. Both horse and rider are inherently "crooked," and this will show up in the saddle as well. I realized this when I put my English saddle on a horse that was "straighter" compared to my horse.

A horse's shape also changes, depending on what it is doing or not doing. When a horse has been out to pasture and isn't being trained, it may lose some muscle and gain weight, whereas a horse that is performing will build muscles. In such cases you can always adjust the padding to fit the horse.

"Work with the horse, not against him.
Always listen to what the horse is trying to say. And always think for yourself."

—Mark Rashid

## Safety

Do not underestimate a horse's need to feel safe. A horse is programmed from day one to survive and will do everything it can to feel safe. That explains why some horses are herd-bound. They feel safer with the herd than with a person.

I experienced this when I first had Riverdance. Until we got the relationship going, she wouldn't venture very far from the stables with just me.

Whenever Hummer came along, she was better—he was a horse, after all, not a human. As time went by and she trusted me more and more, it became easier and easier to go away from the stables alone with her, until one day the issue had simply disappeared.

A horse that feels safe is relaxed and can easily stand still. Often horses cannot stop moving their feet until they feel safe. Just think of horses that dance and prance around when they are nervous.

What is safe from a human perspective isn't necessarily safe from a horse's perspective. How often have I seen riders put pressure on their horses when they refused to do something like go through a puddle or walk past an unfamiliar object? To the human it's only a puddle, but to the horse it looks like a hole in the ground because it can't see the bottom. To the human, it's just a pile of wood, but for the horse this object wasn't there the last time it passed by and thus is unfamiliar.

Having your horse feel safe when it's with you must be a top priority. If a horse does not feel safe, it can never really relax in your presence, nor can it focus on you 100 percent since it has to look out for its own well-being. When a horse feels safe, it's willing to listen to you and is open to learning new things.

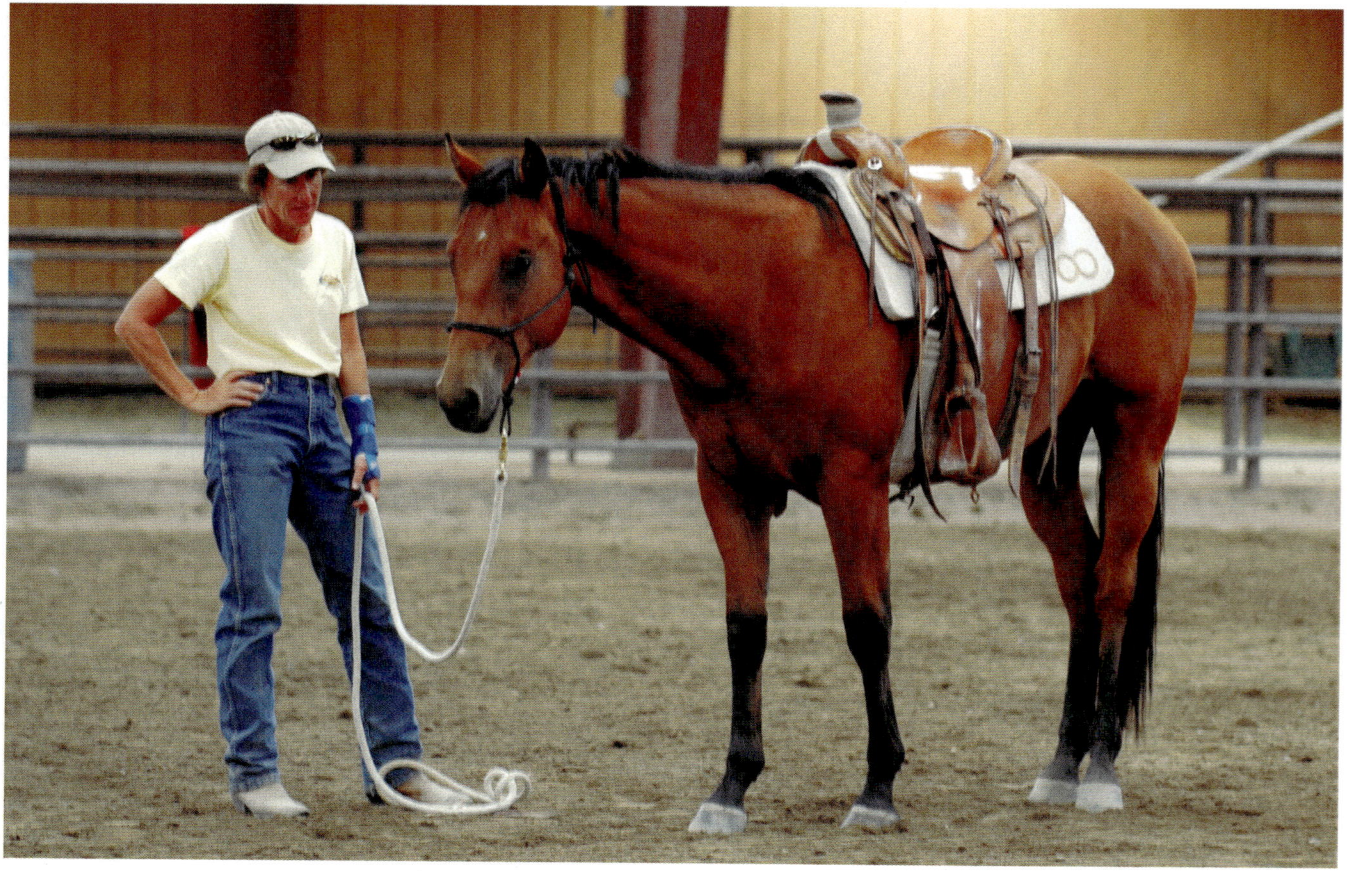

**“I enjoy your company, but just give me some personal space.”**

—Author Unknown

## Space

Horses have their own personal space or bubble around them, just as we humans do. It extends about 4 1/2 feet from a horse's body in all directions. Have you ever watched a high-ranking horse walk through the herd? As soon as it approaches the bubble of another horse, that horse often will move away.

Have you ever noticed how horses respond as you enter that bubble? You will see a change in their body language. Often a horse will turn its head away as your hand enters its bubble to pet it. When you take your hand back again, its head automatically straightens out.

I feel we should ask permission to enter a horse's space. This is especially important when interacting with a horse you don't know. We need to give it the time to permit us to enter its personal space.

It's the same with people. You don't allow just anybody into your space, as the people you let into your personal space determine the quality of your life.

**"We become the stories we tell ourselves."**

—Michael Cunningham

## Stories

Stories distort reality. Stories are only thoughts, after all, and they can unnecessarily worry us when we believe them. Yet stories are the lens through which you view what's taking place with your horse. You add your personal meaning to a situation, and that can unnecessarily trigger emotions.

Let's say your horse isn't picking up the left lead today. How do you respond? "Oh no, not again. I'll never get it right. My horse is terrible at picking up the left lead," or whatever story you tell yourself in this situation.

The fact is, your horse simply didn't pick up the left lead—no more, no less. The "story" is everything you add to what's happened. In most cases, you make the situation worse than it is because you see only the negative in yourself or your horse. Such stories don't put you in the frame of mind to move forward and find a solution, because you are too emotional to think clearly.

It's said that 70 percent of our daily thoughts are negative, so it will require some effort on your part to choose a different response when things don't go well.

Take time to reflect on these questions: What stories do you tell yourself? How do you talk about your horse to others? How do you feel when you believe these stories? How would you feel if you *didn't* believe them? How do you even know whether or not they are true?

I remember Linda Parelli, co-founder of Parelli Natural Horsemanship, saying "My, how interesting" when a horse didn't do something it was expected to do. That was very helpful for me. It left me curious, and I became less emotional. Try it—your horse will thank you for it.

If you are going to tell yourself a story when things aren't going well, why not one that empowers you—like "Hey, I know we can figure this out together."

**"Training a horse is above all feeling and trying, according to what you feel, to help the horse and not to force him."**

—Nuno Oliveira

## Teaching

If you have the chance to observe a herd of horses in a large open area, you'll see how easily and elegantly they move. You'll notice the softness of their movements, their facial expressions. Keep this picture in your mind at all times when you are working with horses. You always want to interact with horses in a way that preserves their natural beauty, expression and dignity. I believe that when we work with the nature of a horse, we can tap into its true potential.

Ronnie Willis said, "Instinct has kept horses alive for over 50 million years. When we teach a horse, we are simply turning its instinctual reactions into responses." That's why it's so important to focus on their mental and emotional states, as these are reflected in the way they respond to us.

Whenever you'd like your horse to learn something new, you want to set it up for success. That means presenting something—such as a new object you want it to walk over—and letting the horse figure out how to do it. I came across a fallen tree one day during a trail ride. I simply gave Hummer a loose rein and the time to sort out how to arrange his feet to get over it, and it went fine. I do the same thing when I place new objects in the arena. I usually have him loose in the arena so he can watch me set things up. I just observe his natural curiosity.

Sometimes I'll put horse treats on the new objects, so he has his own reward when he puts his nose on them. That might be all I will do that day. The second time around I'll set it up again and then just walk around the arena with him on a loose lead rope, not paying much attention to the new things, and let him take note of them as we walk around.

Hummer may even walk up to something on his own, remembering there was a treat there the last time. My goal with teaching is to progress a little bit each time and to ensure that my horses stay motivated.

When teaching new things, remember to stop while you're ahead in order to keep the horse motivated by its own success. So often when a horse does something well, the temptation is to repeat it and ask for even more, but things often go south then and you have to stop out of frustration. In this case, your ego—wanting more and more— simply got in the way.

Perfectionism, another form of ego, can also get in the way. There was a young rider at our stables who typically spent a good hour and a half in the arena. Her poor horse was bored to tears, and she needed the crop to keep her mare going. She was practicing for herself, while the horse had figured things out long ago. To a prey animal born to conserve energy for true emergencies, this made no sense at all.

When I was working on getting Hummer to walk across a carpet in the arena and he did it two or three times, we stopped and moved on to something else, even though this meant stopping well short of the 30 minutes I'd set aside for the exercise.

It's always good to stop while you're still ahead. Resist the temptation to do something "just one more time." If I had continued, Hummer would have seen no point in trying if it only meant more of the same.

Keep in mind that no matter what you do with your horse, you are always teaching it something. You must be aware of what you are doing, because what you allow a horse to do is exactly what you are teaching it. For example, if your horse starts walking and you are not ready but let it continue anyway, then you've just taught your horse an undesirable habit. You've let it take over, not to mention that the horse thinks it's doing the right thing because you are not correcting it.

"If we are impatient, it is because we are concerned with ourselves. When it becomes about the horse, we'll have all the time in the world."

—Mark Rashid

# Time

Only humans have a concept of time and let their lives be dictated by it. This concept doesn't exist for animals. They only know the present moment and simply go with what life brings them in each moment.

Take, for example, a mare and her foal. In nature they live together in a family, a stallion with his mares and their offspring. A foal will be close to mom until she gives birth to her next foal. Even then, the yearling stays in the family and continues to learn about life by living with its family.

Compare this to how a lot of horses grow up in the human world. Most foals never know their fathers, let alone have the chance to learn from them as they grow up. They are often abruptly taken from their mothers at three to six months, breaking the mare-foal bond, to live with other foals for a couple of years until they are trained and sold.

Artificial weaning is one of the most stressful events in a foal's life. This traumatic event, for both the mother and the foal, can have lasting implications. As with humans, traumas leave emotional scars that may not be visible on the outside but can have a behavioral influence later in life.

A majority of the problems people have with horses, both physical and psychological, come about because they put time limits on their horses. For example, you think your horse has to learn to trailer load in the next two months.

Just by saying "My horse has to..." can set up a horse for failure. You are dealing with a horse as a living being, which cannot simply be programmed as you would a machine.

In a world of consumerism and mouse clicks, people expect things to happen instantly. This is not how nature is designed. Nature develops with a perfectly orchestrated natural flow, as when a flower grows and blooms.

We must go with the flow of nature and not against it, as is done in the horse racing business for example, which involves 3-year-olds (9 years old in human years) competing.

What's in it for the horse? A broken body and spirit often are what remain.

Any time you are tempted to put a time limit on something, take a step back and ask yourself if it is really necessary. Is your ego or your heart speaking? Your ego may say, "My horse should know how to do something by this time" or "I should be able to jump three feet by now." Your heart may say, "It would be great to start with trailer loading now" or "It would be fun to jump a bit higher."

Watch your language and how you feel inside; it will tell you whether it's about you or about the horse.

**"Timing is everything."**

—Buck Brannaman

## Timing

Timing is the key to keeping your horse motivated to learn. It's about knowing when to stop, too. To get good at timing, you must to be able to sense where your horse is—mentally, emotionally and physically—in every moment.

In his DVD *Feel, Timing & Balance,* Tom Dorrance demonstrates that everything you need to know about timing comes together when you can balance a broom on your fingertip. What does it take? Give it a try right now!

Foremost, you must *be* in the present moment in order to *feel* what is going on with the broom so you can respond accordingly. Taking *action* at the right moment will keep the broom from falling down. Tom calls it feel, timing and balance.

A lot of the time we can feel that something is off, whether with our horse or in life. If we don't take action at the right moment, things get more and more out of balance.

Timing is important in teaching your horse. If you are asking a horse to load into a trailer and it shifts its focus from looking around to looking at the trailer, reward this effort with positive reinforcement like a praise, a rub, a treat. As a second step, you might reward the horse for shifting its weight forward, even if it hasn't yet taken a physical step. In this case you are rewarding the horse's *intention* to take a step toward the trailer or onto the ramp.

When teaching, you must focus on the horse so you don't miss any opportunity to reward its slightest try.

Timing is also about quitting when the horse is most motivated, so it can't wait to do the same thing when you ask again the next day.

I love chocolate cake, so I use the following analogy when teaching trailer loading. Think about eating a piece of chocolate cake, savoring every bite. If I take it away just as you want to take a bite but then bring you another piece the next day, you'll be eager to eat it.

But if I keep giving you one piece after another, there comes a point at which you'll refuse the cake. Consider this when working with your horse.

If your horse did something well once or twice, stop and build on that the following day.

Our ego often wants more and more when a horse does something well, and that tends to be when things go south. If that happens, it's best to go back to something the horse can do well and feels good about before calling it a day.

Horses are quick learners, or they couldn't survive in the wild. They learn faster than most humans, so a lot of the time we keep repeating stuff for our own sake at the risk of demotivating the horse.

The key to timing is to be so observant and connected with your horse that you simply know when to stop and when to go further to get the change you were looking for.

It's always a good time to stop when you are struggling with your horse. Take a break, do something else, and ask for help if need be.

For some of us, it's hard to stop when we're struggling, because in our mind we feel we have lost and the horse has won. But horses don't know about winning or losing.

How can you tell whether you can move on when teaching? A horse needs time to process what it has just learned before continuing. Once this internal process has taken place, the horse will usually blink, lower its head and chew.

I've found that looking at my horse and waiting for this to happen is counterproductive, though. This is a form of mental and physical pressure, even if we don't realize it.

It's best to step away from the horse and focus on something completely different. I've noticed that the sooner I can focus on something else, the easier it is for my horse to relax and process the new experience.

**"If you have gained the trust of a horse, you have won a friend for a lifetime."**

—Author Unknown

## Trust

What builds trust in you from the horse's perspective? The number one thing is safety. When you can demonstrate from day one that you will never do anything to jeopardize the horse's well-being, it can learn to trust you.

When a horse doesn't trust a human, you can be sure it wasn't born like that. Its experience with humans is what caused this change.

Other important factors for the horse are congruency, integrity and competency. The lack of congruency in the way we communicate often confuses horses, because our actions aren't in alignment with the way we truly feel (see the section on Congruence under the Communication heading).

Integrity means you are dependable because your behavior is consistent and thus predictable. The horse doesn't have to play the guessing game each time you say or do something. Basically, "no" means "no" and "stop" means "stop." If there are too many exceptions to the rule, your perceived integrity will take a hit.

Competency is about capabilities. Your skills and experience will determine your results. Do you have the skills, knowledge and experience you need to achieve what you want with your horse? This applies to all three levels—physical, emotional, and mental.

If emotions still get the better of you, strengthen your capabilities in emotional intelligence, so that you can be the partner your horse needs you to be.

Trust and respect do not begin in the arena. They are part of every interaction with your horse and show up in how you approach a horse, put a halter on, lead it, groom it, saddle it, and how you get on.

Groundwork is also an excellent way to build trust. Basically everything you do on the ground influences the relationship with your horse. And because you take the relationship you have on the ground with your horse into the saddle, this relationship must be built on solid ground.

Take the time to get it right. There are no shortcuts to building trust.

I like to use author Stephen M.R. Covey's analogy of a trust account he uses for the business world. Every action is either a deposit or a withdrawal from the trust account you have with your horse. When the trust account has many more deposits than withdrawals, then your relationship can withstand a challenging situation.

I experienced this with my horse Hummer. I decided to ride through a new area, not realizing that the ground was so soft that his feet sank in. I was afraid that he might start bucking, so I quickly got off and led him through the area, and he trusted me. He was nervous but stayed calm. As we couldn't go back the way we came, we had to go through thick brush to get to the main trail again. I had to take the saddle off so it wouldn't get caught on the branches and Hummer would panic. It was scary for me, because I knew that with one wrong move, we would both be in trouble. Through this situation, I learned a lot about the level of trust Hummer had in me.

A horse that trusts me is a lot more predictable than one that doesn't. I've seen people who want their horses to trust them but have a hard time trusting their horses.

How is the trust between you and your horse? In what situations do you trust your horse? In what situations does your horse trust you? Where is there room for improvement?

**"It's really quite amazing what a horse will do for you, if he only understands what you want. And it's also quite amazing what he'll do to you if he doesn't."**

—Bill Dorrance

## Understanding

Do you really understand what a horse is? How much time have you spent reading about horses, watching films, observing your horse, or maybe even wild horses?

I have spent time on large ranches in the United States, observed wild horses in Bosnia-Herzegovina and have even seen wild mustangs when I was on horseback. These experiences had a powerful impact and helped me get closer to understanding the true nature of a horse.

When I observed the wild horses, I felt the powerful sense of community among them and watched how herds moved as one. It was fun watching young horses play with each other. It was interesting to watch how two stallions interacted when one tried to approach the other's herd. I could easily recognize stallions, not only from their body build, but also from the scars that covered their bodies. I saw how injured horses limped along with the herd, knowing that being left behind would mean death.

It was a peaceful experience because I was there in springtime, after the mating season, when the foals were discovering and exploring the world.

Reading about horses and experiencing them live are two different things, and each has its place. Reading about horses becomes very important when we want to understand more about their physical aspects, such as eyesight. For example, where are the blind spots? How does head position influence what a horse sees, and how does it see in the dark?

Too often we assume that horses are like us, with the ability to adjust from light to dark. But what the human eye can do in seconds can take the horse's eye up to 15 minutes. Once their eyes are adjusted, though, they can see much better in the dark than any human can.

I can only recommend that anyone dealing with horses take more time to understand horses by going out and observing them.

Instead of riding, just hang out alongside the pasture and observe the herd. You may learn more about your own horse in the process.

Today Hummer has his own herd of three mares. In this new role, I saw in him a side I'd never seen before.

When the last mare was introduced into the herd, Hummer became extremely dominant and chased her around the pasture for quite a while before a friend and I stepped in.

That reminded me of Ronnie Willis' saying, "Inside each wild horse is a gentle horse, and inside each gentle horse is a wild horse." You will discover and understand your horse better as you observe how it responds in different situations.

As caretakers of horses, we have a responsibility to treat and work with them in alignment with their true nature.

When I observe the things we do with horses, and how they are stabled and treated, it seems so far removed from their true nature. I believe this happens because we, as humans today, are so far removed from our own true natures and often cut off from our own heart and feelings.

**"To bring out the best in the horse, we need to bring out the best in ourselves."**

—Author Unknown

# Final Thoughts

I have certainly become a better person in so many ways because of who I had to become so that my horses would choose to be with me.

I believe respecting the true nature of the horse and giving it what it naturally needs was also key. Knowing horses spend a majority of their life grazing with herd members, I also built this into our time together and went grazing before or after work in the arena and took breaks during trail rides to graze.

Whenever I ran into obstacles, I saw the horse as a teacher and asked myself, "What do I need to do differently in order for us to move forward together?" As a result, I have been able to progress in my personal development in countless ways.

Horses have given me so much over the years—and for that I am eternally grateful.

# About the Author

Horse wisdom for the human heart best describes Marina's work. She loves to share her passion for horses and what they have to teach people about themselves through her workshops, newsletters, videos and first book, *Leadership Wisdom from Horses.*

Marina is a horsewoman and works as a coach in equine-assisted learning and teaches intuitive riding.

Marina engages readers with her natural down-to-earth style. She writes to inspire others by sharing her insights and personal journey with horses, both as a rider and one whose personality has been strongly influenced by what she has learned through interacting with horses.

For several years, Marina has also been a contributing author for a large magazine for businesswomen in the German-speaking part of Europe.

Marina was born and raised in California and went to UC Berkeley before moving to Switzerland in 1993. She later discovered horses and left the corporate world to pursue her passion for working with people and horses.

Marina now lives in France with her horses and brings a message of transformation and healing as a coach in equine-facilitated learning to her work in Switzerland and France. She loves to spend time outdoors, whether hiking in the Alps, biking through the countryside or playing tennis in summertime. She is always curious to learn more about unlocking the true human potential.

For more information about Marina's work, please go to marinaparris.com

MARINA PARRIS

horse wisdom for the human heart

Made in the USA
Columbia, SC
10 November 2022

70802589R00097